queer eye
FOR THE
STRAIGHT GUY

queer eye
FOR THE
STRAIGHT GUY

The Fab 5's Guide to Looking Better, Cooking Better,
Dressing Better, Behaving Better, and Living Better

**Ted Allen, Kyan Douglas, Thom Filicia,
Carson Kressley, and Jai Rodriguez**

clarkson potter/publishers
new york

Published by Clarkson Potter/Publishers, New York, New York.
Member of the Crown Publishing Group, a division of Random House, Inc.
www.crownpublishing.com

CLARKSON N. POTTER is a trademark and POTTER and colophon are
registered trademarks of Random House, Inc.

Printed in the United States of America

Design by Rob Eric and Jan Derevjanik

Library of Congress Cataloging-in-Publication Data
Queer eye for the straight guy: the fab 5's guide to looking better,
cooking better, dressing better, behaving better, and living better /
Ted Allen, Kyan Douglas, Thom Filicia, Carson Kressley, Jai Rodriguez.
Includes index. 1. Men—Conduct of life.
BJ1601.Q44 2004
646.7'0081—dc22   2003023636

ISBN 1-4000-5446-X

10 9 8 7 6 5 4 3 2 1

First Edition

contents

foreword

Queer Eye was born more than two years ago, one October afternoon in an art gallery in the South End of Boston. Since then, we've been on the ride of our lives. We're the gay/straight duo known as "the Daves"—David Collins, a gay man, and David Metzler, a straight man—who decided that five gay men could bring a sense of style, taste, and class to the lives of straight men.

The story of this show is the story of our friendship. It goes something like this: David Collins was in an art gallery, and David Metzler was at home watching the Patriots lose (this was the pre-Tom-Brady-miracle-season-Patriots, for all you straight guys keeping track at home). D.C. watched as a woman berated her husband for not looking more like the group of fabulous gay men who were standing across the room. She was very animated, making a big point. The fabulous gay men noticed and came over. "Take it easy," they told her. "You've got some great raw materials here. A little pomade, a tuck here, an untuck there—oh, and a nose-hair trim—and you're in business."

That's when it hit D.C.: This was the queer eye for the straight guy. Gay men had something that straight men wanted (well, *needed,* actually). And gay men, working as a team, could give the straight guys—and the women in their lives—what they needed. So D.C. went and told his straight (and, at that time, somewhat disheveled) friend and creative partner, Dave Metzler, that five gay men could transform the world. D.M., sitting on his couch in sweatpants and a ratty T-shirt, covered in Doritos, mourning another Patriots loss, agreed completely.

This was where our journey began. Then it was our friendship that built the show over the next two years, based on a simple premise: Gay or straight, we all want to look better, cook better, dress better, behave better, live better (and have great shoes). And gay or straight, all men are far more similar than they are different. As gay Dave says, "Gay guys, straight guys—they may do things a little different in the bedroom, but in the end, they're still just guys."

Sure, one Dave spends his Sundays at art shows, while the other spends his watching football. One Dave gets pedicures, and one Dave . . . okay, we both get pedicures. One Dave likes boys, and the other likes girls. One Dave says tomato . . . But at the center, where it matters, we're much the same. We've both always wanted the best in life. It's not about materialism (except for the shoe thing), but about the pursuit of excellence, so that your life actually becomes what you dream it can be. It's about believing that everything is possible.

And this optimism may be the core of why the queer eye is valuable, one of the things we find so inspiring about the gay community: There's both an inspiration for and an aspiration to greatness. We don't want to generalize (well, not *too* much), but we've noticed that, for whatever reason, straight men seem much more vulnerable to getting stuck in ruts. So we decided to go out and find them, to pull them out of those ruts and tszuj the hell out of them. It's not about changing them, but about finding the best of who they are and building on that. "You—only better" is the motto of our show.

Finding that "better" within someone is the backbone of *Queer Eye*'s storytelling. From its inception, the show has been about taking viewers on a journey. From hapless to happening, from geek to chic, from drab to fab . . . every straight guy leaves his comfort zone and ends up at a significant destination. He visualizes his potential—and then realizes it. This journey makes us laugh, learn, and often get a little lump in our throat. We're always anxious as we watch the straight guy stumble, and then joyous when he succeeds. We see ourselves in him, in his struggle to be a better man. And so we're rooting for him.

And who better to take a straight guy on the journey of a lifetime than five fabulous gay men? When the Fab 5 was born, they were superheroes in our minds—bigger-than-life gay men, armed with great fashion, good looks, and bottles of eye cream. If there was a straight guy in need, they'd rush to his rescue! Women wished they could have them, men wished they could be them.

Finding these five perfect gay men was an exhaustive process. They needed to be experts in their fields, with innovative approaches to their areas that embodied style, taste, and class; they needed to be smart, with great personalities, and each distinctly funny in his own way. Enter Ted, Kyan, Thom, Carson, and Jai. This team has exceeded every expectation we had. They were instantly as close as brothers, and were indeed the real superheroes we dreamed would save straight America from acid-washed jeans, microwavable food, bad dance moves, hairspray, and futon couches. They truly are the Fab 5.

This show has been a wonderful journey for both of us. Sure, we've changed a little along the way. It's not quite as clear which Dave likes art shows and which one likes football anymore. The pedicures have evolved for both into hot-stone treatments and regular waxings. But the same Dave still likes boys, and the same Dave still likes girls. (Like we said: "You—only better.") It's not gay or straight to want to look good and feel good about yourself (or to have great shoes).

Enjoy the book, enjoy the show, but most of all, enjoy life. That's what having a queer eye is all about.

—"The Daves"
David Metzler & David Collins
Executive Producers, *Queer Eye for the Straight Guy*
New York City, Fall 2003

introduction

In the last year, American men have come to know and expect that the dramatic arrival of five impeccably dressed gay men at their door can mean only one thing: Their life is about to get more fabulous. Hair is going to fly, horrible hetero habits will be exposed and eradicated, ratty futons and plastic flowers will get the heave-ho, the fridge will be carefully decontaminated. He must be torn down before a wonderful new, totally tszujed him can be erected. And you know what? He'll like it. No—he'll *love* it.

We know our mission and how important it is. Every second in America, a straight man puts on a pair of pleated pants. (The shock!) Every minute, a man lathers his bald head with a bar of soap and shaves it with a 29-cent throwaway razor. (The horror!) Right now, in cities and towns across this great land, there are men eating pork-'n'-beans out of can, grooming like Neanderthals, and dressing themselves in the darkness of utter couture-ignorance. (The tragedy!) You needed us, and we were there.

So what does this mean for you? Well, if you're reading this book, you're already halfway to a better you. Because the key to learning how to live a little better is just being open to it—that is, simply, trying. What we talk about in the show and explain in this book isn't highly classified information that's just now being declassified from the archives of the Gay Bureau of Investigation. Women talk about this stuff all the time. Women trade makeup tips and swap recipes and tell each other whose butt looks fat in what. It's just part of their culture, and

Q: Mommy, what's a tszuj?

A: You know how to pronounce it. Spelling variations include *jeuge* (in France), *czuzh* (Russia), and Ted's favorite, *Zhuzhenstraightenguyen* (German, while sipping a glass of crisp Gewürztraminer)—there's a million ways to spell it, and a bazillion ways to do it. Tszujing means taking something and tweaking it, fluffing it, nudging or finessing it to be a little more fabulous and fun. You can tszuj your hair. You can tszuj your sleeves. Watching *Queer Eye* and reading this book can help you tszuj your whole life.

these are things that they're comfortable—and engaged in—discussing. Traditionally, straight men (and, we hear, the occasional gay man from Austria) aren't as open about these things. Why? It's not that they don't want to know. Who doesn't want to know when his butt looks fat? Or how to avoid bleeding when shaving? It's just not part of the conversations straight guys have.

Which is too bad. Because knowing how to dress better, how to behave better, how to look, cook, and live better . . . these aren't girly topics. They're *human* topics. And as we've seen on the show, once you open up guys' eyes to the wonders of hygiene management, a flattering wardrobe, and even perhaps some basic feng shui, they're excited to know more. Teach a man to fish, and pretty soon he's pairing that fish with wild mushroom risotto and a crisp Pinot Grigio. A little tszuj goes a long way!

Perhaps straight guys don't talk about these things because they're afraid it'll make them seem gay. Trust us: no. Just no. Think about the guy you know who cares the most about wine, who dresses sharp, shakes hands properly, and doesn't smell like an athletic supporter. Do you think he worries that his interests seem effete? No. Because he's too busy beating off women with a stick. A little hair gel and some pants that fit aren't going to set off anybody's gaydar, people. Women know who's gay and who isn't, and gay men definitely know. If tomorrow morning you shave correctly and wear a shirt that's actually your size, gay men aren't all of a sudden going to start palming your ass on the sidewalks.

Another thing: A queer "eye" doesn't mean a queer look. It's a point of view, a receptiveness to looking at what works and what doesn't, instead of just accepting things as they are. It's an openness to what's stylish and fun, but not according to any predetermined formula. We don't want you to look just like us. Especially not like Carson. We know that you heteros just can't get away with his particular brand of sartorial splendor. We want you to look *your* best. That means taking who you are, emphasizing the best, eliminating the worst, and tweaking the rest. And that means a process: of checking out what you've already got working for you, what you *can* get working for you, and figuring out how to make that journey from A to B.

Let's repeat that: This is a *journey,* not a firm destination with confirmed reservations for the best penthouse suite. Picking up this book is like buying your ticket; reading the book is like actually taking the first leg. But this isn't the be-all and end-all of every last bit of information and advice on food and wine, grooming, decorating, fashion, and culture. We really are just gay men, not supermen. One book can't cover the whole universe of knowledge—either that we have to offer or that you may want. Ted has hundreds of great recipes in his repertoire; Carson could write a whole book on belts—actually, a whole book just on *buckles*. So don't expect that when you get to the last page, you'll know everything there is to know. You *will* know the basics, and you *will* know what you want to pursue further. You'll know how to take those first steps toward enjoying life to the utmost (and having good hair while you're at it). You'll have a better idea of where you're going, and you'll have fun getting there.

Bear in mind what we always say: *Queer Eye* isn't a make-over show; it's a make-*better* show. Our goal isn't to turn you into someone else. If you're a jeans-and-T-shirt kind of guy, we're not going to make you squeeze into an uptight suit and tie; if you see yourself as a long-haired rock-and-roller, we're not going to tell you to get a Parris Island buzz cut. That's so *not* what we're about. But we *will* find you the *right* jeans and T–shirt, and we *will* make sure your long hair isn't harboring any tangles or aviaries. We're also not going to tell you to go out and spend $70,000 you don't have on a renovated kitchen—or even $7 on a glass of wine you don't want. It's not about spending money, guys: It's about spending *thought.* That's what the queer eye is about, and that's what make-better does.

—The Fab Five
New York City

"Here's the thing:
All you need
to enjoy great food
is an open mind
and the
curiosity and
humility to
ask intelligent
questions."

food and wine

I would like to blame the French. First of all, it is always fun to blame the French, and they've come to expect and enjoy this in their way. Second, I think it falls to the Gauls to accept responsibility for the sorry state of culinary phobia in these Etats-Unis. They are superior cooks and they will never let anybody forget it. They persist in christening their wineries with names that we can't pronounce. And with their super-Frenchy domination of all things tasty, it might appear that they have cowed the average American guy into believing that food and wine are impossible for mortals to master and are best left to specialists. French specialists.

But actually, it's our fault. Even now, after years and years of surging interest in cooking and eating well, I believe we are still largely a nation far too intimidated by cuisine. And it is decidedly our loss.

Oddly, we embrace the foodstuffs that we actually should fear: the processed, the prepackaged, and the artificially preserved. But when it comes to such happy things as exquisite restaurants with dazzling silver and wineglasses the size of a baby's head, an amazing number of Americans—men and women, straight and gay—are so intimidated they would rather eat deep-fried "blooming onions" in chain restaurants alongside shopping malls. Personally, I think our bad eating habits—and our fear of changing them—have a lot to do with the circa-1950s haughty fine-dining experience. It's an outmoded cliché that we still hold to as truth: the snooty maître d', the vast and bewildering wine list, the dress code, the fussy presentations, and, simmering beneath it all, the deeply held suspicion that French people are making fun of us for not knowing their luxurious language, and sticking us with bad wine for enormous amounts of cash because we're too ignorant to know the difference.

Let's make a few pronouncements, shall we? Excellent. Great food and wine is about having a great time. It's about celebration. It's about learning new tastes and interpretations of classic ideas. It's about putting delicious things in our mouths. Even kids and dogs understand this. Why can't grown men? There's almost no better way to learn about other cultures than through their foods, almost no better way to get to know people with your clothes on. But first and foremost, it should be about enjoying life with friends and family, and about having fun. Food should never *not* be fun. And it's been my experience that the vast majority of people who dedicate their lives to the exceedingly difficult business of working in 100-degree kitchens all hours of the night actually feel that way about what they're doing. They love food. They love people—at least, they love people who also love food (and who tip well). They are generous people, even if their corkage fee is a little steep. So fear not the saucier, the sommelier, or any of those other French-sounding gatekeepers of good taste.

Why are so many men inept at how to behave in a nice restaurant, let alone at attempting to whip up a sole meunière at home for their Special Lady? The French aside, I think it's perfectly understandable. Many of us don't know much about food, which is a natural consequence of nobody ever teaching us anything on the subject. Because baking pies and cookies is still considered girly in some corners. Because it's seen as fussy to appreciate a beautiful entrée delicately composed in a puddled sauce on a plate, when what a "real man" supposedly wants is a bloody four-pound porterhouse. Because the world of wine is vast and bewildering even if

hiptip

If you're going to a party and you're bringing a bottle of wine as a host gift, it's really nice to buy something unique, something that you can't find in every supermarket. Better to tell the clerk at your wine store your budget and ask him to give you something unusual. It's fun for him, a little challenge, and makes you look good with the host.

you do know the difference between a Château Y'Quem and Thunderbird. You know, in a book with "Straight Guy" in the title, the old cliché about men being too proud-slash-insecure to ask for directions was bound to come up sooner or later. So let me be the first to raise it: Guys are too proud-slash-insecure-slash-hardheaded to ask for instructions in the realm of eating well. Enough, already. Time to let that anxiety go and have something to eat.

The waiter is your friend. The wine guy, whatever he's called (it's actually pronounced *so-mahl-ee-ay*), he's your friend too. Think of them as guides, like the grizzly and sunburned types who take you deep-sea fishing. You wouldn't go deep-sea fishing without a grizzly and sunburned type. So why think you should be able to intuitively wow your colleagues with an encyclopedic knowledge of Bordeaux?

Here's the thing: All you need to enjoy great food is an open mind and the curiosity and humility to ask intelligent questions. Here's the other thing: Being open-minded and curious is sexy and interesting, unlike being stuck in your ways, which is not. And another: Sooner or later, women have to eat. If you like that sort of thing—women, I mean—you're going to need to take them to restaurants and (if you're smart) cook them dinner once in a while. And you're going to want to look cool in the process.

So, herewith, our introductory guide to eating well, one of the hallmarks of living well. *Bon appétit*—or, as they say, Good eatin'!

getting
started
food's got rhythm

Fruits and vegetables, for those of you unfamiliar with the concept, are nature's delicious, prepackaged, ready-to-eat snackstuffs conveniently sprouting from the ground or dangling from low-hanging trees. But you should know that vegetables, like beer, are best consumed at the peak of their freshness. Think of them as having "born-on dates." And realize that just because supermarkets sell tomatoes all year round doesn't mean they're fit to eat—most of the year, in fact, they're not. If McDonald's sold the Shamrock Shake all the time, it wouldn't be so special, would it? Just as Shamrocks are at their McFinest in March, real tomatoes (that is, those that ripen in *actual* sunshine) are at their peak in July, August, and September. Take a look around a farmer's market or local produce stand. This is the stuff that's good right now—fresh and in season.

vegetable peak pickings

apples	September to November
artichokes	March, April, May
asparagus	March, April, May
cantaloupe	May to October, with the peak in July; the rest of the year they look the same but taste like cardboard
corn	July to September (if you need to have corn other times of the year, buy frozen sweet corn)
green beans	April to October (but don't be afraid to use frozen)
honeydew melon	August to October; the rest of the year they are almost inedible
peas	April to June (but unless you're cooking them a few hours after picking, frozen peas are almost as good)
peaches	May to October
pears	August to early spring
plums	May to October
spinach	March to April, September to October
tomatoes	July to September
watermelon	June to August
zucchini	May to July

straightguyFAQ

Q: If I can get produce year-round, why do I care what's in season?

A: Because out-of-season produce tastes lousy and never has the texture you want. A dish is only as good as the ingredients you put into it—substandard veggies will actually do harm to whatever it is you're making. A February tomato, a zucchini in November, or a peach in April are likely to be mealy and flavorless. You *can* get decent out-of-season fruit, flown in from other continents, but it's harder to find, more expensive, and less reliably good.

the essential tools

ten culinary weapons every man should own

8-Inch Chef's Knife

The most important tool in any kitchen, period. Everything needs to get cut, and this is the guy to do it. Tall enough so you can chop without slamming your knuckles onto the cutting board. Other knives come in handy for specific tasks—a serrated knife for slicing bread, a carving knife for that holiday bird, a paring knife for, say, peeling mangos. But a good chef's knife will get you through 95 percent of your cuts with aplomb, and the other 5 percent in a pinch.

Instant-Read Thermometer

Nothing produces more anxiety in the kitchen than the issue of undercooking or overcooking the turkey. Or the $15-per-pound beef tenderloin. And nothing is more easily solved—without cutting into your roast. Spend five bucks on a simple instant-read thermometer, consult a meat-temperature chart for the desired doneness, and bring some precision to the pork roast.

12-Inch Tongs

In the pantheon of kitchen tools, these are the jaws of life. Grab, flip, stir, twirl. The best. They allow you to turn meat without puncturing it (and hence without losing all of the juices that make meat tasty), they're great for moving things around in a pan, they're easy to use, and they'll make you look like more of a pro than any four-thousand-dollar stove.

10-Inch Sauté Pan

The all-purpose pan you'll use every day. Spend the money on solid construction and quality—from high-quality brand names like All-Clad or Calphalon, for example. You want one with an aluminum core, which conducts heat better, for more even cooking. And throw away all those college-era tin pans you have rusting up the joint.

The Sturdy Roasting Pan—with Handles

Great for roasting chicken, potatoes, prime rib, and leg of lamb. And since you'll probably have no other space to store it but in the oven, it will keep your oven thermometer company. An oven thermometer, by the way, measures the temperature in your oven (it's a different thing from your instant-read thermometer, which is for food).

Dutch Oven or Enamel-Coated Cast-Iron Pot

The most carefree, hearty entrées are those made in the following fashion: Put a bunch of meat and vegetables in a big pot with some liquid, and let it cook slowly for the better part of a day. In order to make these, you need a big, heavy pot, preferably made of cast iron and coated in enamel (a reasonably nonstick surface). Get a big one—say, 8-quart—and fill it with the aforementioned ingredients now. We'll be right over.

Pepper Grinder

Freshly ground black pepper is a must for almost any savory (that is, not sweet) dish. I'm partial to the little cast-aluminum jobs with a crank handle on top—fifty bucks, but they last forever.

Cast-Iron Grill Pan

Not just another pan, this is the power of barbecuing harnessed for indoor, off-season use. The ridges give meats and vegetables distinctive grill marks, and the seasoned surface means no sticking and, therefore, easy cleanup. Knocks the George Foreman on its ass.

Digital Timer

Make that *two* timers. Especially when you're juggling multiple dishes. You won't want to be doing sums on your forearm to coordinate this stuff.

Rubber Jar Opener

Sure, you're a strong, masculine guy. Powerful forearms and all that. But wouldn't it be humiliating if you tried to open that jar of cute little French cornichons . . . and failed. *While she's watching.* It can happen to anybody—sometimes those lids seem practically soldered on.

Q: I know how to treat a lady. How do I treat a cast-iron pan?

A: To keep a cast-iron pan happy and nonsticking, don't let it soak—it will rust—and don't use soap. Just sponge with warm water. If there are stuck-on bits and you need something abrasive, try kosher salt. (Really.) After each rinsing, put a few drops of vegetable oil on a paper towel, and rub the inside of the pan all over, to create a thin, shiny film. (Really: You *want* oil in this.) If you buy a new cast-iron pan, follow the directions that come with it, to season it properly.

straightguy**FAQ**

More Essentials

Cheese grater If you're into pastas, you need this for your parmesan, if nothing else.

Vegetable steamer For quick-cooking vegetables while retaining all their flavor, color, and nutrients—and, let's face it, if you're going to eat broccoli, you want those nutrients—nothing beats steaming. This is an insert to a bigger pot, and works like a charm.

Mixing bowls Get a good set that stacks together and doesn't take up much cupboard space. My favorites are made of Pyrex, an extra-sturdy glass, or stainless-steel models with rubber, non-skid coating on the bottom.

Kitchen shears Formally, these are used mostly for things like removing the ends of chicken wings and cleaning uncooked soft-shelled crabs. But once you get used to the fun of a combination scissor-knife, you'll find that it's a great way to snip herbs, carve a bird, and even divide up a pizza.

Essentials, Plugged-In

Food processor If you really get into cooking, this will, sooner or later, be indispensable for speeding up chopping tasks and for making sauces and dough.

Blender If for no other reason than frozen cocktails.

Coffee grinder The number one secret to superb coffee is fresh-ground beans—as in, freshly ground this second, right before you make the coffee.

Rice cooker Despite the extraordinarily easy instructions on every package of rice, it's oddly difficult to get it perfect. Available in supermarkets, hardware stores, nearly anywhere with kitchen-supply departments, and even Asian delis, rice cookers ensure success.

mixing bowls

5-inch serrated utility knife

6-inch boning knife

8-inch slicing knife

8-inch chef's knife

9-inch bread knife

6-inch cook's knife

4^1/$_2$-inch sandwich knife

3^1/$_2$-inch utility knife

"Cooking is like shaving: It's no fun without a sharp, *sharp* blade."

sharp insight: knives to know

Cooking is like shaving: It's no fun without a sharp, *sharp* blade. You can't really accomplish anything in the kitchen unless you have good knives. You can have cheap cutting boards, cheap bowls, but if you're going to enjoy cooking, you need good steel. Buy Henckels or Wüsthof, both high-quality German numbers, available at any store with a cookware section (as well as any cooking-oriented catalog or website). Or, if you don't mind washing them by hand, the good old wood-handled Chicago Cutlery. Better to buy one or two really expensive do-everything models and just get a cheap bread knife (anybody can make a serrated knife that is going to work fine—that's the sledgehammer of knives). Many of the high-end models have plastic handles, a plus here, because it allows them to be put in the dishwasher. (Take note of the converse: Wood implements of any sort should *not* go in the dishwasher—your cutting board, salad bowl and serving spoons, those wood-handled steak knives you got for Christmas from your father-in-law . . . none of them goes in the dish-washer. Ever. The hot water and soap will ruin the finish of the wood and, worse, make it swell and crack.)

In addition to your chef's knife, get a paring knife or two. If word gets out that there's a hetero man in the kitchen and you're bombarded with gift certificates from elated aunts, buy another chef's knife in another size—a 10-inch, say—for variety's sake.

To keep your knives sharp, give them five or six strokes on the sharpening steel every time you use them. You'll still need to sharpen them professionally, at a store with a good cutlery section, every year.

nothing says love like a cocktail

Is there anything better than a cocktail? I mean, other than love and peace and all that? Love, peace, and an ice-cold cocktail: If anything beats it, I haven't tried it, and it's probably not legal. There's a reason why they call it "happy hour." Vodka, in particular, makes a lot of people happy. I don't know if that's because it's flavorless (so that even people who don't like the taste of liquor can drink it) or because some people are under the impression that it's lower in carbohydrates than other spirits (so the Atkins-dieter can drink it). Yes, it's the slimming, healthy spirit. It's made of potatoes—it's practically a side dish.

But my favorite drink is the classic gin martini. Not new, not trendy, but then again unsurpassed for elegance and simplicity and style. Whatever your drink, the great thing about cocktails (other than social lubrication, relaxation, and pretty colors) is that there are so many kinds to drink and so many fun times to try them. Stock your bar at home and learn to mix the classics for friends. Find a new favorite and impress the ladies with an exotic order. Cool people are always drinking a new drink. To help you keep up and to ground you in the basics of mixology, here are a couple recipes (one classic, one Queer Eye exclusive) and a year's worth of drink ideas.

two
drink
recipes,
one
great
hangover

martini

There are as many martini misconceptions out there as there are bastardized recipes. I'm not a huge fan of the "chocolate martinis" or the fig-gorgonzola-eucalyptus-methadone martinis that have popped up on a lot of menus in the last couple of years. I also happen to believe that a martini should actually have vermouth in it. A lot of people think the best martini is the driest one, with as little vermouth as is humanly possible. They'll dab a drop of vermouth on their pulse points, or merely think of the word *vermouth* and call it a martini. Listen: A martini can be anything you'd like it to be, but a real one has vermouth in it. Like this:

2 ounces gin

1/2 ounce dry vermouth

Green olives to garnish

Start with room-temperature gin (see Hip Tip, page 32). Pour it and the vermouth into a cocktail shaker with ice and shake until your hand feels frozen and frost appears on the outside of the shaker. (You're serving this drink straight-up, meaning without ice, so you want it to be as cold as possible.) Strain into a martini glass and garnish with an olive or two—on a silver pick, if you want to get fancy.

straightguy FAQ

Q: How many martinis to have?

A: A straight guy once told me that martinis are like women's breasts: One's not enough, and three is too many.

fire island iced tea

Put down that cosmopolitan and back away slowly. The cosmo, as a British actor once told me, is awfully poufy. Herewith, a new drink that's refreshing and bracing and just gay enough (I mean, *rose*mary?). Delicious!

1 1/2 ounces vodka (see Hip Tip, below)

3 ounces rosemary-infused lemonade (see Note)

Splash of Cointreau

Splash of unsweetened iced tea

Sprig of rosemary, for garnish

In a pitcher, stir the vodka, lemonade, Cointreau, and iced tea and pour over ice in a highball glass (a tall, skinny glass). Garnish with a sprig of rosemary.

note: To make rosemary-infused lemonade, dissolve 1 1/2 cups sugar in 1 1/2 cups hot water, add a few sprigs of rosemary, and let steep for 30 minutes to an hour, depending on how much you want to taste the rosemary. Discard the sprigs and mix with 1 1/2 cups fresh lemon juice and 2 1/2 cups cold water.

Contrary to popular belief, gin and vodka shouldn't be stored in the freezer. Water is actually the unheralded secret ingredient of a good shaken cocktail. When you shake or stir a nearly frozen spirit with ice, the alcohol doesn't warm up the ice, and not enough water melts into the drink, resulting in a drink that's too strong. Yes, there is such a thing: A mixed drink should *not* taste like fire and make your eyes water; it should taste like heaven and make your eyes warm. Crazy but true.

hiptip

5 Keys to a Successful Cocktail Soirée

1. Get the essentials. Your guests can live without watermelon liqueur and pomegranate schnapps. They will riot without vodka and other basic boozes (see "Bar Essentials," page 34).

2. Buy the good stuff. Life's too short to drink cheap booze. If you must cut costs, use the lesser brands for mixed drinks, and save the good stuff for drinking straight (so to speak).

3. Have a "signature drink." Find a drink you love to make and push it gently—people love to try new tipples.

4. Prep like a chef. If you know you're going to be mixing a drink with a lot of lemons or limes, cut a bunch of them ahead of time to avoid congestion at the bar. Here's the best way: Cut off both ends and discard. Set the fruit on one end. Cut it in half, and then cut each half in half, and then cut all these pieces in half again, and you have perfectly acceptable wedges.

5. Serve your guests solids. As much as you want everyone to have a ball, you don't want them asleep under your sink before dinner. At the very least, put out nuts, chips, or other simple bar snacks. See pages 39–40 for some good basic recipes.

be prepared: bar essentials

There are lots of specialty liquors, liqueurs, mixers, and gadgets that you don't need for a cocktail party. How many urgent requests for a sloe gin fizz do you think your guests will make? Zero. Here's what you *do* need.

hard stuff Vodka, gin, bourbon, scotch, and rum (light rum is more universally appealing than dark or spiced rum). And tequila, if you run with that type of crowd.

liqueurs and aperitifs Dry vermouth if you expect even *one* martini drinker. It's nice to have an aperitif like Lillet or Campari around too. Everything else is pretty much optional, for specialty drinks.

wine and beer One type of white wine and one type of red; I like to go for a light, crisp white such as Pinot Grigio and a fruity (as in tasting like grapes) red like Zinfandel. And then a full-bodied beer such as Sierra Nevada Pale Ale, plus a light beer. Even if you don't drink light beer, many women and men (gay and otherwise) do; if any of these creatures are coming to your shindig, try to make them feel welcome.

tools If you want to project any degree of class whatsoever, you'll need something other than a plastic bucket to hold ice. For example, a ice bucket. Preferably with tongs or a large, long-handled spoon. You'll also need a corkscrew and at least two bottle openers (if your beer isn't twist-off): Nothing goes missing at a party quicker than the one bottle opener you have. And at least one cocktail shaker or pitcher.

mixers Tonic, club soda, ginger ale, cola, cranberry juice, orange juice. Pineapple or grapefruit juice if you're feeling tropical. And sparkling mineral water. Always go for fresh, not-from-concentrate juices. Remember that some people—designated drivers and pregnant women, for example—may actually be drinking this stuff straight.

garnishes No, I'm not going to tell you to practice setting lemon peels on fire to drop, flaming, into martinis. (Though that's awfully fun.) But I am going to tell you that *every* mixed drink looks a lot more appetizing with something solid thrown into it or perched along the rim. Even if all you're going to do is cut a bunch of limes and lemons into wedges or slices, do it. Have a jar of pitted olives at the ready. If you want to get fancy, and have a conversation piece also, get some mini-cocktail onions. When someone asks what they're for, say, "It's the right garnish for a gibson, my house drink." (A gibson is a martini garnished with a tiny pickled cocktail onion instead of an olive or lemon peel.)

ice Buy far more than you think you'll need. If you buy it (or, better yet, have it delivered) right before your party starts, you don't need to keep it in the freezer—a clean sink, big pot, or nearly any other container will do, and a big bag of ice will keep itself cold, unrefrigerated, for hours.

emergency-hour plastic cups Preferably sturdy, clear ones without any cartoon characters on them. Even though you're serving out of proper glassware—you *are* using glass—sooner or later, you'll probably run out of the real stuff. So have decent plastic around.

Q: I'm constantly running across "simple syrup" in drink recipes. What is it?

A: It's a way to sweeten drinks. Sugar doesn't dissolve well in cold or even room-temperature liquids, and you don't want gritty grains in your drink. To make simple syrup, combine equal parts sugar and water in a small saucepan. Heat over a medium flame, stirring with a wooden spoon, until the sugar dissolves. Let cool, then store in any container with a tight-fitting lid. It will keep, refrigerated, for a few weeks.

A Year of Drinking Well

Twelve months of cocktail inspirations, and not a modified martini among them.

january
Irish Coffee

The perfect New Year's resolution killer, this warmer-upper has everything: alcohol, caffeine, sugar, and richness. Cool.

      Coffee

      Sugar

1½ ounces Irish whiskey

      Whipped cream, for garnish

Fill a mug, preferably a clear glass one, halfway with coffee. Add sugar to taste. Pour in the whiskey, stir, and top with whipped cream. Serve with a spoon.

february
Daiquiri

It's winter in the States, but it's always summer in Cuba. The classic daiquiri isn't slush that's piped out of a frozen-drink machine into a blue-tinted plastic novelty glass garnished with 120-decibel hip-hop. It was Hemingway's drink when he lived in Cuba, and it should taste like fresh lime juice and rum, not an adult-rated Slurpee.

2 ounces light rum

1 ounce simple syrup (see page 35)

¾ ounce fresh lime juice

In a cocktail shaker, shake all the ingredients over ice. Strain into a chilled cocktail glass and garnish with nothing except your pride in serving a *proper* daiquiri.

march
Cuba Libre

The politically incorrect way to say "rum and Coke." If you ever find yourself at a White House reception, order this loudly, and watch the Secret Service draw a bead on you.

2 ounces rum

   Coca-Cola

   Lime wedge

In a tall, skinny glass (called a highball), pour the rum over ice. Add Coke to taste—2 ounces will make a strong drink, 6 ounces a weak one. Squeeze in the lime wedge, and serve. Note that the lime juice is critical here.

april
Mimosa

It's tough to beat champagne at breakfast.

2 ounces orange juice, preferably fresh-squeezed

4 ounces champagne or other sparkling wine

Pour the OJ into a flute or wineglass, then top with the bubbly.

Mint Julep

Official drink of the Kentucky Derby, run on the first Saturday in May. Hangover should lift by Memorial Day. Not so much minty as it is bour-bony and strong.

- ½ ounce simple syrup (see page 35)
- 2 sprigs of fresh mint, well-rinsed
- 2 ounces bourbon

In the bottom of a highball glass, muddle the simple syrup with one of the mint sprigs (that means crush the mint in the bottom of the glass, using the handle of a wooden spoon). Fill with crushed ice, add bourbon, and stir with a spoon until frost forms on the edge of the glass. Serve with the other sprig of mint as a garnish. If you fall in love with this drink, or get involved in the horsey set, try to find yourself some julep cups at a flea market or antiques store: They're made of silver and hold 8 or so ounces of liquid. They will set you apart as a true julep connoisseur and man of the world.

june
Margarita

In the past couple of years, fancy añejo (aged) tequilas seem to have bum-rushed the United States like an army of crazed mariachis. Leave those complex, fine-sipping bottles on the shelf when you make a margarita—their subtle nuances would just be overpowered by the other ingredients.

- 1½ ounces tequila
- 1 ounce Cointreau
- ¾ ounce fresh lime juice
- Salt, for rim of glass

In a cocktail shaker, shake all the ingredients (except salt) over ice. Sprinkle the salt onto a small plate (a saucer should do it), and rub a piece of lime around the outside rim of a cock-tail glass. Dip the moistened rim into the salt and it will stick. Strain the liquids into the glass and serve.

july
Pimm's Cup

The official drink of Wimbledon. Be the first person at your local dive bar to get dirty looks for ordering this oddity. It's made with a gin-based aperitif called Pimm's #1 (there are other Pimm's numbers, for aperitifs based on other liquors), which is a combination of gin and aromatics.

- 2 ounces Pimm's Cup #1
- 3 to 4 ounces homemade or high-quality store-bought lemonade
- Club soda (or champagne, to go really upscale with this)
- 1 cucumber

In a highball glass over ice, combine the Pimm's Cup #1 and the lemonade, stir, and top with soda (or champers) to taste. Stir again. Peel the cuke. Cut off and discard the ends. Cut it in half lengthwise, then quarter each half, creating eight long spears. If the cucumber was long and these spears are unwieldy, cut them in half. Garnish your drink with one. Eat the others, lightly salted with a squeeze of lime, to fortify you for the long day ahead.

august
Gay Kool-Ade

Or so it's been dubbed by a certain maverick TV producer. (Word, D.C.!) Sans the splash of cran, it's Straight Kool-Ade. (Cheers, D.M.!) It's hot out, so no time to be a discriminating drinker. Cheers, queers!

Vodka

Club soda

Merest hint of cranberry to color

No time to be a discriminating mixer either. Whatever proportions feel right to you, in whatever glass you please. You're "versatile," right?

september
Cosmopolitan

The cosmo may be oh-so-very-1998, but it's still oh-so-popular. You should know how to make one correctly.

1½ ounces citron vodka

Splash of Cointreau

¼ ounce fresh lime juice

1½ ounces cranberry juice

Lemon peel, for garnish

In a cocktail shaker, shake all the ingredients over ice. Strain into a chilled cocktail glass and garnish with a lemon peel.

october
Manhattan

Some people prefer Manhattans with whiskey or rye; I like mine with bourbon. All are correct—liquor choice is at your discretion. But you need sweet vermouth (which is not the same stuff as you put in a martini), and you need bitters, which are like Worcestershire sauce for cocktails.

2 ounces bourbon

1 ounce sweet vermouth

2 dashes Angostura bitters

In a cocktail shaker, combine all the ingredients over ice and shake until it's all very cold, about 30 seconds. Pour into a chilled cocktail glass (a.k.a. martini glass). The traditional garnish is a maraschino cherry, but that's up to you.

november
Hot Toddy

Not so much a cocktail as it is chicken soup for the imbiber's soul. You can use brandy or rum, or brandy *and* rum.

½ ounce brandy

½ ounce fresh lemon juice

Hot water or hot tea

Sugar, to taste

In a mug, combine the brandy and lemon juice, and top with at least 3 ounces of hot water or tea, more if you're feeling peaked, and add sugar to taste. Pull off those ski boots and tell untrue stories of how you conquered the bumps today.

december
Champagne Cocktail

A cerebral, celebratory fizzy drink to end the year.

Angostura bitters

½ ounce simple syrup (see page 35)

Champagne

In a tiny, tiny bowl, pour a few drops of bitters over a small ice cube. Let the excess drip off the cube, then drop the bitters-laced cube into a champagne glass. Add the simple syrup, then top with champagne, slowly, until the glass is full.

bar snacks

Making sure your guests have something to nibble on is crucial, not to mention hospitable. It can make a casual get-together more elegant. It keeps people from sopping up too much booze too quickly. One-on-one, it can be a great way to establish a little intimacy before heading out to a crowded restaurant. Dim the lights, put on some good music, and riff off on some of the recipes below. Or, in a pinch, **imported olives** (not the jarred kind, but from a deli counter) never let a man down; for greater crunch, consider the Japanese wasabi pea: different, spicy, green. Both of these can just be served straight from the store, at room temperature, in little bowls.

Five Easy Pizzas

Take lavash (an unleavened Middle Eastern flat bread) and top it very lightly with shredded mozzarella and a range of simple ingredients of your choosing, below. Bake at 400°F. for about 7 minutes. You could even use a good toaster oven for this, if you cut the bread first.

one. Caramelized onions: In a large skillet over medium-low heat, sauté 1 thinly sliced onion in 2 tablespoons extra-virgin olive oil for 30 minutes, until soft and browned.

two. Crumbled hot Merguez lamb sausage (or other spicy sausage): Remove from its casing, crumble, and sauté in a dry pan for 10 minutes over medium heat, until cooked through.

three. Sliced fresh mushrooms and a drizzle of white truffle oil (available in specialty markets) or extra-virgin olive oil.

four. Halved cherry tomatoes with shreds of fresh basil.

five. Pieces of very thin asparagus and prosciutto (you could put this stuff on shredded wheat and it'd still taste good).

Q: I like to do shots. Is there something wrong with this?

A: Yes. For the same reason that nobody needs to be drinking beer with a tube and a funnel. There's something wrong with rapidly ingesting as much alcohol in as short a time as possible with the aim of getting as drunk as possible. That said, a shot can be fun. But call it a "shooter" instead of a shot, and make it out of a mixed drink instead of pure alcohol. You still get to toss it back like a pro, but without the desperate adolescent feeling.

straightguyFAQ

Spiced Nuts

Sugary, spicy, and highly addictive. Put 2 cups of pecans, walnuts, or a combination of the two in a nonstick skillet over medium-low heat. Stirring constantly, add 1/2 cup of brown sugar mixed with 1/2 teaspoon salt, 1/2 teaspoon cinnamon, 1/4 teaspoon ground cloves, 1/4 teaspoon ground allspice, and 1/4 teaspoon cayenne pepper. Keep stirring until the sugar starts to melt, 5 to 10 minutes. Take the nuts off the heat immediately and spread over foil to cool. Sprinkle with more sugar and spice. Serve at room temperature.

Parmesan Crisps

These are delicious, they make your house smell amazing as they bake, and anybody can make them. Sprinkle 2 tablespoons of finely grated parmesan (*not* the stuff in the can, but from the refrigerated cheese section of a supermarket or from a cheese counter at a good food shop) on a baking sheet in little 3-inch ovals. Add a grinding of black pepper and, if you like, some chopped rosemary, sage, or thyme. Bake for 8 minutes at 350°F., until golden brown.

Ridiculously Simple Canapés

Brush extra-virgin olive oil on cocktail-size slices of dark rye bread (available at most supermarkets). Top with prosciutto, some shredded arugula, and a few strips of parmesan cheese (use a vegetable peeler to create an attractive cheese curl).

Basic Glassware

There's a world of glassware out there, but don't worry too much about brandy snifters and pousse-café glasses (glasses designed especially for a drink called, no kidding, a pousse-café). You don't need them. Buy a set of rocks glasses, some taller highball glasses (you'll also use these for juice and soda), and invest in one cool piece, like a vintage pitcher or a chrome shaker. You can get great deals on stylishly retro barware at flea markets. You'll put your over-ice or neat drinks (vodka and ice, scotch, etc.) in the rocks glasses, and almost everything else in your highballs.

Cocktail glasses are mandatory for cosmos or martinis—the stems keep your hands from warming the drink. Bonus: They can double as elegant servers for fruit or chocolate mousse.

wine
what it is

The world of wine can appear so vast and overwhelming that a lot of guys just avoid it completely. And that's because there are approximately eighty-seven billion different wineries producing eight hundred trillion varieties, many of which are labeled in French and referencing confounding geographic minutiae. It's a vast landscape, often overseen by people with foreign accents. Then there's that off-putting veneer of elitism, one-upsmanship, and enormously high prices.

Why would a man feel intimidated by that?

Please trust me that these days it's not as bad as all that. Relax. Nobody is expecting you to acquire the palate (or the outfit) of a master sommelier. You don't need to know that much about wine to enjoy it. Wine should be about fun and celebration and maybe dancing and looking like a bit of an idiot (but not too much) and regretting it in the morning (the dancing, not the wine).

So we're here to demystify. It's only fermented grape juice with a funny name. That makes people laugh louder. And can complement everything from steak to hake, whatever the hell hake is.

Wine makes a great gift, especially when you make it personal. This is what I do for my sister, who lives in a part of the Midwest that's not exactly the wine crossroads of the world: Around Christmas every year, I go to my favorite wine shop with $100 and ask the salesman to pick six bottles—three reds and three whites. Dealer's choice. I want him to dazzle me with fresh, new, interesting finds, and tell me what everything is. I write down these descriptions and send them to my sister with instructions like, "This one's for roast chicken . . . " She loves it, I enjoy it, I get one relative scratched off my list—and I learn a lot along the way.

hiptip

Queer Eye is all about giving guys license to ask other guys for help. As a gender, we hate doing this. If you're reading this book, though, you're man enough to appreciate some guidance. So pick a sommelier at a restaurant you like, and enlist him to be your guide in the exciting world of viniculture. He will be pleased—it is a compliment to be asked to share expertise. This is his calling. Most sommeliers are not there to rip you off or sell you the most expensive bottle on the list. They have better things to do. And I can assure you they make their real money on the movie stars who order the really expensive stuff.

The Ritual

It helps to know a bit about what to expect when you order wine. It's a simple little game. They bring you a wine list, you pick a wine. You ask your wine steward—or whatever hapless drama major they've cast in the role of keeper of the wine list—what would taste good with what you want to eat. Give him or her a price range. If you're on a date and you don't feel like enunciating dollar amounts, just point at a dollar figure you can handle and say: "She's having the snapper; I'm having the grouper; we'd like a wine that would taste good with both and we're thinking something like *this*." Point to the "$15" or "$22" or whatever it is you're cool with. They'll get it. They know you don't want to look cheap. And you don't want to look like a show-off, either: "Give me any wine you got for $200!" Don't do that. If you don't know what you're talking about and hope that throwing money around will cover for you, you'll just end up looking like a jerk.

The Delivery

Next they'll show you the bottle. This is so you can confirm it's the one you asked for. (It always is, but you *should* check the label.) Next, they'll open the wine at your table—in front of you so you can be confident they're not going back in the kitchen and pouring Château Merde into an expensive bottle. Then, they may present you with the cork. Contrary to popular misconception, you are not to smell it—there's no point to that whatsoever. What you do is this: You *read* it. It should be imprinted with the same brand as on the label. (This ritual was clearly invented by wine lovers who didn't trust waiters.) Or you can just ignore it.

Want to swirl wine in your glass like a master? Practice this at home: Hold the stem of the glass with the ends of your thumb, index, and middle fingers, as you might hold a pencil. (In fact, *always* hold your wineglass by the stem, both to avoid warming the wine and to keep the glass free of fingerprints.) Now imagine you're drawing small, tightly concentric circles on the table with the glass. Do this *slowly,* and make the circles *small.* (High speed or large ovoids may result in sloshing.) If your circles are too small and too slow, nothing much will happen, so increase their size a bit and wait for results; it takes a few rotations to get the swirl going, which, in turn, stirs up the aromas. Smell is the major component of taste, so it's an aspect of the wine experience that you might as well enjoy.

hiptip

The Tantalizing Taste

Now they'll pour a small amount of wine into the glass for you to sample and make sure the wine is in good condition. A lot of winos like to swirl it around to get the wine moving in the glass, which releases more aromas. What they're looking for here—other than just enjoying the "bouquet"—is to see whether the wine's been "corked" or ruined by air leaking in or improper storage or a bunch of other things you really shouldn't worry too much about. If it's corked, it will smell moldy, or taste like vinegar, or be revolting in some other fairly obvious fashion. If you think there's something terribly wrong with it, ask the wine steward to taste it. Seriously, these are people you can trust.

At any rate, feel free to fake the swirl-and-smell bit. Two words of advice, though: Don't over-swirl or you could slosh onto your date's blouse, and don't draw out the time it takes to sniff and squint into the glass before you nod your approval (about as long as you could hold the direct gaze of a stranger is a good guide). So: Taste it, and if you have real concerns, let the server know. This is not the time, however, to decide you really meant to order a red instead of a white. And the point here isn't for you to assess whether you really love the wine—it's to assess whether the wine is in good condition or not. Play fair with the restaurant and give the wine a chance, too. It will "open up" a bit—change its taste as it stretches out, gets used to being out in the air after being cramped up in that bottle.

straightguyFAQ

Q: **What do I need to know about vintages?**

A: Knowing when a wine was made can tell you a lot about its character, history, and value. But knowing that the vast majority of wine produced on the planet is made to be consumed right now, without aging, is probably more important for the beginning wine drinker. So don't get distracted by all the numbers when there's a world of great wine ready for drinking today. (That said, when in doubt, 1997 was one of the best years in recent memory for reds.)

know your grape

Ever notice when you're out for dinner with a group, everybody tries to foist the wine list off on somebody else? Nobody wants to make that call. But once you realize that you really only need to know just a few good wines, it all becomes easier—both to order what you know and to have a conversation with the waiter or sommelier (the guy in charge of the wine list) about what you're unfamiliar with. If you can keep in your head five good reds and five good whites—the winery names as well as the types of wine—that are all readily available and frequently found on wine lists, you'll be an instant dinner hero. Here are ten wines I really like.

Five Whites to Know

Sauvignon Blanc A grape name, best from France, California, New Zealand. From tart and citrusy to creamier, more I-Can't-Believe-It's-Not-Butter varieties, goes well with seafood and chicken. Good value found in the New World (that's wine-speak for "not Europe") varieties, especially New Zealand. Lighter and crisper than big, bold Chardonnay.

Gewürztraminer A grape name that's as German as it sounds. Floral and fruity. Can be cloyingly sweet but the dry ones are delicious—notably those from Alsace, such as Pierre Sparr and Trimbach. Great with Chinese and Thai food.

Champagne A place—and a happy place indeed—where our French brothers make the most famous sparkler. Not only is the bubbly for more than just special occasions, it's actually delicious with food. A brut (dry) sparkler is perfect with savory hors d'oeuvres, and a demi-sec (slightly sweet) is an amazing complement to Indian or Asian dishes.

Pinot Grigio A grape name (also known as Pinot Gris, in France), mainly from Italy. Important yet simple Italian varietal; light, crisp, refreshing. The official wine of summer, tailor-made for sipping on balmy evenings.

Chardonnay From all over, but most come from California, France (especially Burgundy), and Australia. The most popular white wine in America, but you should know that it's pretty bold and can overpower the delicate flavors of many foods.

Five Reds to Know

Cabernet Sauvignon Probably the most popular red grape in the U.S., producing great wines in California, and is the main grape in the noble wines of Bordeaux, in France. It's a big, bold, intense varietal. If beef is what's for dinner, Cab is what you're pouring.

Cabernet Franc A vastly underappreciated grape, from France. Perfect with lamb or the Thanksgiving turkey. Lighter than Cabernet Sauvignon. Earthy, herbal.

Syrah A grape also called shiraz by the winemakers of Australia; it's an earthy, full-bodied red that often has spicy flavors. Try it with duck or other game.

Pinot Noir A grape name, primarily from France and the United States. (Just as Chardonnay is the primary white grape in Burgundy, Pinot is the primary red.) Complex, high acidity, big grape. Look for it from Oregon on domestic wine lists, or French Burgundies.

Zinfandel Indigenous to California. Jammy and robust. It's become a big-deal wine, though values are still out there.

Wine: How to Learn More

The way to learn about wine is not through a mail-order course or a big book of flowcharts and diagrams. The best way, and the most agreeable, is to learn one bottle at a time.

Keep tabs If you try a wine you love, write down the name of the grape, the maker, and the year it was produced. This is an especially good idea if you tried a wine you loved with a certain dish (Pinot Gris with seared snapper, the Valpolicella with Charlene from Accounting, etc.).

Shop till you drop Wine stores are like Booze Universities. Find one with a good vibe, and get to know the people who work there. These people are not to be feared. You know, there are a lot of easier ways to make money than selling wine. People who sell wine do it because they love it. And they're great resources: They know their stuff and they'll teach you about wine, no charge. Tell them what you're making for dinner and ask what would go well with it. Talk to them about the occasion, the mood, what you've tried recently and liked or hated. A lot of shops host free tastings—a great way to try before you buy.

Read, selectively Wine books tend to be dull and confusing. A better way for the layman is general-interest or men's magazines that write about wine occasionally. They tend to have straightforward advice and buying suggestions—for example, they'll just say here are ten great bottles of wine to drink right now.

Share with friends If you really want to give yourself a little crash course and you don't want to read a book and don't like classes, tell your wine-store guy that you're going to do a tasting and get a selection—either all of one variety of grape, or different things you'd like to try together. Invite your dorky friends over for an "informative" tasting party. No uppity wine experts. Just you and your friends getting a little geekier together.

the romantic dinner

a survival guide

Ah, the Romantic Dinner. Fancy restaurant. Candlelight tête-à-tête. Strolling violinists. Elaborate food you wouldn't let your buddies see you eating, at painful prices. More strolling violinists. Ill-fitting tie, stalled conversation, the sudden need to burp. Just you and your sweetie . . . in an emotional bear-trap ready to snap. This isn't the way is has to be, or should be, but this is the fear: Yes, there's something about the Romantic Dinner that just seems fated to go badly. Partly it's the weight of doing something out of your ordinary routine, something probably expensive and unfamiliar and high-stakes and contrived. So the pressure builds—you *must* have a good time. And it builds to the point where you really *can't* have a good time. Which is a damned shame for several reasons: (a) it's just dinner, and dinner involves eating and drinking, which we've learned are fun; (b) women do not like to have their bubble burst; and, finally, (c) it just doesn't have to be this way.

The thing to remember is: It's just you and your date. Do not be intimidated by the situation, by the large volumes of extraneous silverware or the pressure to suddenly exude the charm of George Clooney. Try to relax and enjoy yourself. Barring that, learn to fake it.

Garlic Is Not the Problem
5 Things Not to Order on a Date

Spaghetti Bolognese Slurpy, splattery, and dangerous around expensive shirts and ties. In fact, any type of long, strandy pasta with any type of sauce is pretty risky.

Fried chicken Greasy and nearly impossible not to eat with your hands, which is rarely an attractive sight.

Spare ribs Same reason as above, plus the whole man-gnawing-on-bone thing, which is a little Cro-Magnon.

Veal Dead baby anything is not the best program for a love connection. This goes double if the menu specifies it as baby veal. Ouch.

Lobster Avoid, unless you're both ordering it. Nobody looks good in a bib.

how to avoid heartache at the table

Sure, we'd all rather be sucking back beers and watching the game (or figure-skating, as the case may be). Odds are so would she. (And maybe with someone else.) But the Romantic Dinner is an inescapable fact of the mating life. So you might as well learn how to avoid some of the pitfalls.

Don't Order for Her

Enough said. Unless she's hoarse from berating you on the way over for not asking for directions, let her do her own talking.

Wine, not Whine

If you don't know anything about wine, don't make a big deal about this. Don't sweat at the sight of the wine list or weep at the prices. Be cool. It's just a beverage. A beverage that increases the chances she will laugh at your jokes. And if you do happen to have an encyclopedic knowledge of wine, keep it to yourself. She doesn't want a lecture at dinner and will be much more impressed with effortless interaction with the sommelier and a quick return to paying attention to her. Remember, she's what you're there for. Keep your eye on the prize.

Return to Sender

If you do drink a lot of wine, sooner or later you're going to come across a bottle that was spoiled in storage. Ninety-nine times out of a hundred, if you alert your server to your concerns, he'll be gracious about it and immediately procure another bottle. That said, most people who send stuff back to the kitchen are usually just doing it because they want to make a scene.

However, if something *does* go terribly wrong—if someone is rude to you, or none of your food arrives, or if it arrives cooked incorrectly (you asked for rare and you got medium-well), or someone accidentally flambés your girlfriend's ponytail—stand up for yourself. But do it in a polite way. Being a jerk is the last way you're ever going to impress your date or enjoy the meal you're spending all that money on.

cook
for her

Here's the secret: You can't go wrong cooking for your love interest. You just can't. Do the chicken right and she will do you right. And if you burn the chicken? It's cute. An anecdote. As long as the entire house is not consumed in flames, you will not merely endure the trials of cooking for a woman, you will prevail.

All you have to do is try. Find some recipes that will go well together—find them in a cookbook, download them from the Internet (I love Epicurious.com), get them from your mom, clip them from a magazine, or use the ones in this book. Follow the instructions as close as you can, but don't be too fussy about it—cooking is an art and a science. Allow yourself plenty of time; dinner guests, like feral animals, can smell panic, and it makes them uncomfortable. Put on some music while you work. Open a bottle of wine and have a glass. (But take it easy—drunk cooks have a tendency to lose the tips of their fingers.)

Relax. Have fun. Eating food you cooked yourself—and feeding it to someone you care about—is fun. Because it doesn't matter if the food is perfect; the point is, you tried, *for her.*

contemporary comfort food

Lemon-Rosemary Roast Chicken

Zucchini and Yellow Squash Julienne

Mushroom Risotto

Cinnamon-Walnut Baked Apples

lemon-rosemary roast chicken

The Queer Eye is all about tszujing—about taking a classic and injecting it with a little something extra, a little thought and effort. This recipe is your classic roast chicken, tszujed. Unless you're feeding a vegetarian, you can't go wrong.

serves 4

4 1/2-pound roasting chicken

1 lemon, quartered and zested (see Hip Tip)

1 1/2 tablespoons chopped fresh rosemary, plus several sprigs for stuffing and garnish

1 teaspoon kosher salt

1/2 teaspoon freshly ground black pepper

2 garlic cloves, minced (optional)

1/4 cup extra-virgin olive oil

2 large onions (about 1 pound), quartered

Preheat the oven to 350°F.

Rinse the chicken inside and out, then pat dry with paper towels.

In a small bowl, combine the lemon zest, chopped rosemary, salt, pepper, and garlic (if using). Dump half this mixture into the cavity of the chicken, along with the flesh of the lemons and the sprigs of rosemary.

Add the olive oil to the bowl of seasoning, and whisk with a fork, forming a paste. Massage this mixture all over the outside of the chicken.

Place the onions in the bottom of a roasting pan—the heaviest roasting pan you own (and It would be nice if it's also nonstick). Set the chicken breast-side up on the onions, and put in the oven. Bake for 1 hour, basting occasionally if you remember to, by using a long-handled spoon (or, better yet, a baster, if you have one) to retrieve the juices from the bottom of the pan and pour them over the top of the bird.

Raise the oven temperature to 400°F. and roast until the skin browns a bit, about 15 minutes. Carefully turn the chicken, using tongs or long-handled forks, so the breast faces down. I don't want to scare you here, but if you're not careful about this, there may be some hot-oil spattering, which has the potential to ruin your shirt or, if you're going short-sleeved here, give

hip tip

The tszuj: Substitute lime zest for lemon to get a more Caribbean aroma and flavor. Also try thyme instead of rosemary, or use both.

Herbs

Loosen up with herbs. When it comes to most cooking (not, mind you, baking, which is a very precise endeavor), we're talking more right-brain than left. The amounts of ingredients you use can often be adjusted to your personal taste. And nowhere is this more true than with herbs. You can usually substitute one herb for another, particularly if a recipe sounds great to you but contains a strong herb that's not your favorite—say, replace mint or tarragon with basil, cilantro with the milder flat-leaf Italian parsley, or rosemary with thyme. Success, of course, will vary, too. You have to experiment, and you have to taste. Not sure what those bay leaves are doing to your recipe? Put one in your mouth and chew on it. Then you'll know.

you little hot-oil burn marks on your forearms; not a good thing, and painful too. So proceed with caution, and maybe even wear those oven mitts your mom gave you when you moved into your first apartment.

Continue to roast for 30 to 40 minutes, until the skin has browned and crisped. Remove from the oven and let rest for 10 minutes or so before carving. This isn't an 18-pound turkey, so you're not going to be doing any fancy slicing here: Just find the natural joints that'll divide the chicken into 4 quarters—2 thigh-leg combos, 2 breast-wing—and push apart with a knife. Serve with the onions on the side. And if you think you or your date doesn't want to eat the onions, think again. Give one of these a try. They just cooked for 2 hours while being continually basted with herbs and chicken fat. Sweet and delicious.

hiptip

Citrus zests are one of my favorite kitchen secrets. (Why? See the next pages.) The zest is the outer layer of the citrus rind, the part with the texture and color. (The inner layer, called the pith, is white and bitter; you don't want this.) To get the zest, rub the fruit along the smallest holes of a box grater, being careful to leave the pith on the fruit.

I use citrus zests—
lemon, lime, orange,
even the occasional grapefruit—
all the time in cooking,
and also in cocktails.
They provide
fresh, potent citrus
aromas and flavors.
And they give you the
opportunity to use a fancy
chef's phrase when your
guests ask you why something
tastes so special: Say, a little
offhandedly,
"Oh, I just freshened it up with a
little lemon zest."
Freshening up a dish or a drink
is providing that extra little tszuj.

zucchini and yellow squash julienne

Have you ever noticed that Chinese restaurants can bring a stir-fry to your table thirty seconds after you ordered it. Ever wonder how? The secrets are that the ingredients are prepped ahead of time (called *mise-en-place*) and cut small, so they'll cook quickly. That's how this recipe works. *Julienne* is a fancy name for "thin strips," which cook quickly and evenly, and allow you to easily control their texture—a few seconds less cooking for the firmer crunch that I prefer, a few seconds more for a softer veggie, and a few minutes more if you're trying to re-create the soggy mush that your junior high school cafeteria specialized in.

serves 2

1 small zucchini

1 small yellow squash

1 teaspoon kosher salt, plus more to taste

1 tablespoon extra-virgin olive oil

1/2 teaspoon chopped fresh oregano leaves

Freshly ground black pepper to taste

Trim the ends of the zucchini and squash, and cut each lengthwise in quarters. Lay each quarter on the cutting board, and cut into long slices, about 1/8-inch wide; try to keep your slices as even as possible. When you're done, cut across all these strips. You should now have a whole mess of strips, 1/4 inch wide and about 3 inches long. This is your julienne.

Put your julienne into a large colander, sprinkle on the salt, and let it sit for 10 to 15 minutes. The salt will draw out some of the moisture—all squashes contain a lot of water, which is one of the reasons they're often soggy. Not good. Squeeze out as much of this water as you can—just get your hands in there and squeeze—and then pat dry with paper towels.

In a large nonstick skillet, heat the oil over a high flame until hot, about 1 minute. Toss in your julienne and cook, stirring nearly constantly, for 2 to 4 minutes, depending on what consistency you want. Add the oregano and salt and pepper to taste. Serve hot.

Q: Cutting all those strips of vegetables sounds like a pain. Any alternatives?

A: If you have a food processor, the strips will take less than a minute (using the finest-cut slicing disk). If you don't, and you're not willing to do this with a knife, this recipe will also work with rounds: Just cut the zucchini and squash into very thin (1/8-inch) rounds, and cook another minute or two. But the great thing about the strips is how cool it looks.

mushroom risotto

Ah, risotto (pronounced "ree-zoh-toe"). A great alternative to pasta or potatoes, this Italian rice dish will show you're a true man of the culinary world. Risotto can be as simple as rice and broth, or it can be a complex amalgamation of seafood, vegetables, and a handful of herbs. I prefer something in between, balancing just one major taste against all the creamy rice. You can substitute any kind of wild mushrooms, here—just don't use the bland white ones. And don't add too many ingredients: The rice is the co-star.

serves 4 as a side, or 2 as an entrée

6 cups (1¹/2 quarts) low-sodium canned chicken broth, or boxed organic broth

3 tablespoons extra-virgin olive oil

¹/2 pound portobello mushrooms, stemmed, cleaned, and thinly sliced

¹/2 pound cremini or button mushrooms, stemmed, cleaned, and thinly sliced

1 medium onion, finely chopped

1¹/2 cups risotto-style short-grained rice (varieties include Arborio and Vialone Nano; do *not* use varieties that aren't specifically intended for risotto)

¹/2 cup dry white wine

2 tablespoons unsalted butter

¹/4 cup chopped fresh chives

¹/2 cup freshly grated parmesan cheese

Salt and freshly ground black pepper to taste

On a rear burner of your stove, in a small pot, heat the broth to just below the boiling point. Turn the flame to very low and keep at the barest simmer.

On the burner in front of your broth, heat 2 tablespoons of the olive oil in a large nonstick skillet over a medium-high flame. Add the sliced mushrooms and cook, stirring often, until they've wilted and released their juices, about 5 minutes. Empty the contents of the skillet—mushrooms and oil—into a small bowl.

In the same skillet, add the remaining tablespoon of oil and warm over medium heat. Add the onion and cook, stirring often with a wooden spoon, until totally wilted but not browning, about 5 minutes. Raise the heat to medium-high, add the rice, and cook, stirring, for 3 minutes; the rice will take on a little bit of color, but be careful not to let it stick to the bottom of the pan and burn.

(recipe continues)

Pour in the wine and stir until it is absorbed by the rice, about 1 to 2 minutes, stirring all the while. Once the wine is gone, repeat the process with the warm broth—add 1/2 cup at a time, stir, and wait for the liquid to be absorbed before you add the next 1/2 cup. Keep stirring as much as you can bear. Continue this for a total of 15 to 20 minutes of broth additions, until the rice is cooked through but still a little firm (al dente) to the bite. You may not need all of the broth, and the end result should be *slightly* soupy—just a little liquid among the grains of rice.

When the rice is done, return the sautéed mushrooms to the pan. Stir in the butter, chives, and parmesan, and add salt and pepper to taste. Cover the pan and let it sit for at least 2 minutes, then serve immediately.

Precooking Risotto

This recipe, along with nearly every other recipe for risotto, keeps you in the kitchen for about a half hour before eating. This creates the ideal risotto, but not the ideal date—you've got better things to be doing when your date is wandering around your apartment, possibly discovering your "private reading material." And although chefs won't readily admit it, this also isn't how most restaurants prepare their risotto—it takes too much last-minute cooking.

Instead, do this: Cook the risotto ahead of time for 12 or so minutes, until the rice is getting softer but still a little too firm to eat. You should have 2 cups broth left over. Spoon the nearly cooked rice out of the hot skillet and onto a cookie sheet, spreading it as thin as possible to dissipate the heat and halt the cooking. Cover with plastic and refrigerate.

Then, when it's time to eat: Bring 1 cup broth to a boil in your risotto-cooking skillet. Reduce the heat to medium-low, add the cooled rice, and stir furiously for 1 to 2 minutes, until the broth is absorbed. Then continue adding broth in 1/4-cup increments, until it's done to your satisfaction, and proceed with the endgame of the recipe. You'll still need to leave your date alone, but it'll be for just 5 minutes, not 25.

Q: What's with this talk of "al dente" as pertains to pasta?

A: *Al dente* is Italian for "to the tooth," meaning that pasta and even some rice—as in risotto—is best when it's not overcooked, when it still presents the slightest resistance as you bite into it. It's not an exact science; cooking times will vary depending on the size of the pot you use, whether you're cooking in Denver or Death Valley or in the galley of a 747 at 35,000 feet. You have to taste as you go: Stick that pasta fork in there every minute as the suggested cooking time comes close, blow on the noodle or rice real quick, and give it a chew. You don't want it tough or chalky; just slightly firm.

straightguyFAQ

Other Risottos

This basics of this recipe—sauté onions and then rice, then cook with slow additions of wine and broth, then finish with cheese—can be a template for nearly anything you want to throw into the mix: shellfish, meats, vegetables. Prepare these elements in another pan until they're cooked, then add to the finished rice. Here are some favorite combinations:

Peas and prosciutto Couldn't be easier. Microwave a box of frozen peas, slice up a few ounces of prosciutto, and add to the cooked rice.

Saffron The most expensive spice in the world—ounce for ounce, it costs more than nearly anything—is the secret to the famous Risotto Milanese. Just dissolve $1/2$ teaspoon saffron threads in $1/2$ cup of hot broth, let it sit 10 minutes, then add to the nearly finished rice. The yellow coloring, heady aroma, and unmistakable taste of saffron turns ordinary risotto into a fragrant, beautiful side dish.

Mussels or clams When the rice is done and sitting, steam mussels or clams just until they open. Dump them into the rice, stir, and serve.

Parmigiano-Reggiano

Real parmesan cheese—called Parmigiano-Reggiano in Italy—does not come in a green cylindrical container. It comes in tremendous drums that weigh a legal minimum of 53 pounds—that's right, legal: In Italy, they regulate cheese (not to mention wine and cured meats and even pizza) with the same conviction that we legislate our tax code. You can buy wedges of it as small as a couple ounces, or you can buy it pregrated. But please: Buy the real thing. And, at least once, try buying a wedge of it, instead of grated, and take a nibble. Or two. And then drizzle on some good aged balsamic vinegar and have another nibble. And maybe pair it with a nice ripe fig . . . now we're talking. Many people consider Parmigiano-Reggiano to be the world's greatest cheese—sweet, nutty, floral, with a great granular texture.

cinnamon-walnut baked apples

Comfort food at its finest. Plus, you prepare everything ahead of time. When you serve your entrée, put the prepared dessert in the oven, and it'll be ready when you are.

serves 2

 2   sweet apples, such as Fuji or Jonagold

1/4   cup chopped walnuts

 1   tablespoon light brown sugar

1/2   cup maple syrup

1/4   teaspoon ground cinnamon

1/4   teaspoon ground nutmeg

    Zest of 1 orange (see Hip Tip, page 55)

 4   tablespoons unsalted butter

    Crème fraîche or whipped cream, for serving

Preheat the oven to 350°F. Cut the apples in half through their equators. Using a paring knife or a spoon, remove the cores. Cut a small slice out of each end so that the apples will sit flat.

In a small bowl, combine the nuts and sugar. Pack this mixture into the apple halves. In a small saucepan, bring the maple syrup, cinnamon, nutmeg, and zest to just a boil, then add 2 tablespoons of the butter and stir until it melts.

Find a baking dish—the smallest one you have that accommodates all 4 pieces of apple with at least 1 inch between pieces. Spread 1 tablespoon of the butter around the inside of this dish. Put the stuffed apples in it, and pour the maple-syrup mixture over and around the apples. Top the apples with the remaining tablespoon of butter, sliced into 4 thin pats. (At this point, you can put the baking dish in the fridge, covered in plastic wrap. When you put your entrée on the table, take off the plastic and place the dessert in the oven.)

Bake for 30 to 40 minutes. If you think of it, use a wooden spoon to baste the apples a couple of times with the syrup mixture that will have pooled in the baking pan. If you don't think of it, don't worry about it. Allow to cool for 5 or so minutes before serving, with dollops of crème fraîche or whipped cream on the side.

Pan-Seared Scallops in Brown Butter Sauce

Asparagus Glazed with Balsamic Vinegar and Olive Oil

Herbed Israeli Couscous

Mocha Granita

seafood, but fresher than fish

pan-seared scallops in brown butter sauce

Scallops: tender, sweet shellfish, but without the shells. The healthful, fresh taste of the sea, but more special-occasion than, say, cod. And they're incredibly easy to get right, with just a few precautions: Get them completely dry before cooking, make your pan really hot, and don't crowd the pan. Oh, and most important: Don't overcook. Scallops are best lightly cooked—that is, still a bit soft and moist in the center.

serves 2

8 large fresh sea scallops (about 1 pound)

1/2 teaspoon salt

1/4 teaspoon freshly ground pepper (preferably white, but black will do)

5 tablespoons unsalted butter

1 tablespoon extra-virgin olive oil

2 tablespoons chopped flat-leaf parsley

Juice of 1/4 lemon (about 1 tablespoon)

Using paper towels, dry the scallops until every last bit of surface moisture is removed. Sprinkle on both sides with the salt and pepper.

In a large, heavy skillet over medium heat, melt 1 tablespoon of the butter with the olive oil. When the foam subsides, turn the heat to high and let the oil get nice and hot. Using tongs or a spatula, carefully add the scallops to the hot pan; they may hiss and spatter, but not too much if you did a good job of drying them. Each scallop should be at least 3/4 inch from any other and from the sides of the pan.

Cook the scallops, without harassing them—no pushing, no nudging—for 2 to 3 minutes, until a nice brown crust appears underneath. (Check by just angling one scallop a little out of the pan.) Turn and cook the other side for 2 minutes, again until there's a nice crust. With tongs or a spatula, remove the scallops to 2 warmed plates (see Hip Tip, page 72).

Reduce the heat to medium and add the remaining 4 tablespoons of butter. It will foam, then turn a nice nutty brown color within a couple of minutes. Add the parsley and lemon juice, give it a swirl, then pour the brown butter—which you can now feel free to call *buerre noir*—over the scallops on each plate. *Et voilà!* Serve immediately.

hip tip

If you can find bay scallops in season, especially Nantucket bay scallops, buy 'em—they're sweet as candy! The smaller bay scallops should be cooked a total of 2 to 3 minutes, stirring frequently, until lightly browned.

asparagus glazed with balsamic vinegar and olive oil

If you need to serve a green vegetable—and you do, unless you want your guests to develop anemia—asparagus is one of your better bets. Almost everybody loves it for its sweet, nutty flavor (in season, of course), it's great-looking on the plates, and it's really easy to cook.

The thick root ends of asparagus are tough and should be removed before cooking. Luckily, each spear of asparagus comes with its own trimming instructions, courtesy of Mother Nature: Hold the very butt of the root end with one hand, and firmly grasp the other end just below the spiky tip. Slowly but firmly bend the spear, and it will snap—just at the point that divides the tough part from the tender part. This spot is different for each spear, so do these one at a time; it takes just a few seconds apiece.

serves 2

2 tablespoons extra-virgin olive oil

$1/2$ pound asparagus, trimmed (see headnote) and cut on the bias (that's diagonally) into 2-inch pieces

2 tablespoons balsamic vinegar

$1/4$ teaspoon Dijon mustard

$1/2$ teaspoon sugar

Salt and freshly ground black pepper to taste

In the largest skillet you have, heat the olive oil over medium heat. Add the asparagus and cook, stirring occasionally, until tender but still a little firm to the bite, 3 to 4 minutes. Using a slotted spoon, remove the asparagus to a small bowl. Add the vinegar, mustard, and sugar to the pan, increase the heat to high, and let it boil away for 1 minute, until it thickens slightly. Return the asparagus to the pan, season with salt and pepper to taste, and serve.

Q: Do I need an expensive, aged balsamic vinegar?

A: It is better, and can approach such sublime perfection that it's hard to believe it is a vinegar. If you're using balsamic vinegar for drizzling purposes—as the sweet balance to a hunk of nutty, salty Parmigiano-Reggiano (see page 61), for example, or even to give vanilla ice cream a kick (which actually is great when you use the ultra-sweet, twenty-five-year-old kind of vinegar)—get the best stuff you can afford. But if you're going to be cooking with it or using it with other ingredients in a dressing, the supermarket variety will suffice.

straightguyFAQ

herbed israeli couscous

First of all, Israeli couscous is not just a kosher version of regular couscous or anything like that. Also labeled Jerusalem couscous in some quarters, it's a different dish altogether than the Moroccan variety: a much larger grain, like a little ball bearing about half the size of a green pea. Better yet, these little pasta-like beads have a terrific texture; cooked properly al dente, they pop in your mouth. Perhaps best of all for new cooks (or cooks on the go), it's an interesting side dish that is very versatile and incredibly easy to prepare; much more foolproof than rice, say. If you don't have chicken stock, you could also cook the couscous in water with a teaspoon or so of salt, as you often would with pasta or rice (see below). But using the broth infuses the dish with terrific flavor without adding fat or anything else bad for you (use this trick with mashed potatoes, green beans, almost anything you choose to boil). As for the thyme versus dill question, it's a matter of taste; dill is quite a strong herb, so I prescribe less of it than thyme, but I like it as a foil to the nutty, brown-butter sauce and rich flesh of the scallops.

serves 2 to 3

1 cup canned low-salt (or, better yet, homemade) chicken broth

1 cup Israeli couscous

1/2 teaspoon sea salt

Pinch of freshly ground black pepper

1 teaspoon fresh chopped thyme leaves, or

1/2 teaspoon chopped fresh dill

Bring the broth to a boil in a medium saucepan. Turn off the heat, add the couscous, cover, and let stand for 12 minutes. Fluff with a fork, add the salt, pepper, and thyme or dill, and that's it: Serve. Didn't I tell you it was easy?

Q: If I'm using salt and butter in a recipe, why use unsalted butter? Why not have the salt built in?

A: Over- and under-seasoning are the most common mistakes home cooks make. You want to be in complete control of your salt additions—you can always add it, but you can never take it away. So have salt on hand, and add it in small increments. Don't rely on your ingredients—especially butter and broth—to provide the salt, because they may provide too much of it.

mocha granita

Granita is the authentic version of an Italian ice, and this coffee-flavored one is a specialty of Sicily. This is a cinch to make, and of course it freezes well, so the yield is for 4. Have any leftovers for breakfast.

serves 4

3 cups extra-strong coffee

2 ounces chocolate syrup

1/4 cup sugar

1/4 cup half-and-half or whole milk

While the coffee is still hot, stir in the chocolate and sugar. Add the half-and-half and let cool to room temperature. Place a baking pan in your freezer and pour in the mixture. After 30 minutes or so, as it starts to freeze, scrape it off the sides and stir with a fork to break up the ice into tiny shards. Put it back in the freezer, let it firm up again, and break it apart again. Repeat every half-hour, 2 or 3 more times, until the ice has formed a smooth, evenly frozen solid.

When it's time to serve, do it in style—in little espresso cups with little espresso spoons. (Or at the very least, in cute little bowls. If you're unsure of a given bowl's cuteness, ask a gay guy.) *"Prego!"*

hiptip

Taste, taste, taste. Taste your food throughout the cooking process, for several reasons. One, it helps you learn what's happening to the dish as it goes through its stages. Two, it keeps you apprised of whether there's enough salt, pepper, etc., in the food. Three, it's the primary fringe benefit of being the cook; that and having easy access to the wine.

Simply Steak

Twice-Baked Potatoes with Cheddar
and Caramelized Onions

Hot, Garlicky Swiss Chard with Almonds

Gooey Chocolate-Coffee Brownie Cake

steak 101

simply steak

"Buy the best ingredients you can find"—it's what every chef, magazine, or cookbook will tell you over and over again, about everything. That's never more true than when you're investing in steak. Sure, maybe that London broil is only $4 per pound. But if this is a special meal, cheap meat is not what you're looking for. If you can find it, buy dry-aged beef. I love bone-in rib eyes and porterhouse, but everybody has a favorite cut. Look for well-marbled meat, which means you can see ribbons of fat running through it. Without this fat, you don't have flavor (which is why tenderloin may be tops for texture, but *not* for taste). You're not looking for anything that says (or looks) "lean." If lean is the goal, buy some halibut.

You might notice that I'm not grilling our meaty treats in this instance, as much as I love char-grilled goodness. Reason: I figure some of you live in apartments, and it's occasionally wintertime. But also, pan-searing actually lets the flavor of the steak shine through even better, without masking it with smoke.

But speaking of smoke: Crank your exhaust fan up to high for this recipe; otherwise, you'll trip the smoke detector. And it's hard to look cool while you're fanning smoke away from the smoke detector.

serves 2

2 high-quality steaks, each about 10 ounces and 1 inch thick

1 tablespoon kosher salt

1 tablespoon freshly ground black pepper

1 tablespoon extra-virgin olive oil

1 tablespoon unsalted butter

Preheat the oven to 450°F.

Season the steaks on both sides with the salt and pepper, then massage in the olive oil with your fingers. Heat a large, heavy skillet (preferably cast-iron; see page 23) over high heat for 3 minutes, until very hot. Add the butter When it melts, add the steaks. Let them sizzle away for 1 1/2 minutes per side. Transfer the skillet to the oven, and cook for 6 minutes for rare, 8 minutes for medium-rare. If you think you like your meat medium, think again, and try it medium-rare. If you think you like your meat well-done, think again: You don't actually like meat. Beef is not tasty well-done; it just isn't.

Carefully remove the skillet from the oven, wearing an oven mitt. (Remember, the handle is 450° too!) Remove the steaks from the pan, put them on a plate, and cover with foil. Let them rest 5 minutes before serving. *Do not skip this step.* It's crucial for meat to rest after the cooking is done, which allows the juices to redistribute throughout, making each bite as moist and tasty as possible. If you serve it without the resting period, the juices will run all over the plate when you make your first cut. Nobody likes a dinner plate to look like a crime scene.

herbed butter

Want to be a little decadent? Serve with a pat of melting butter on top of your steak. Want to be really decadent? Serve with a slice of herbed butter. Ahhhh . . .

1 stick unsalted butter, softened

1/2 teaspoon minced fresh basil

1/2 teaspoon minced fresh chives

1/2 teaspoon minced fresh oregano or marjoram

1/4 teaspoon salt

Pinch freshly ground white pepper

In a small bowl, combine all the ingredients and mash together with a fork. Dump the butter onto a large sheet of plastic wrap and roll it up into a cylinder, $1^1/2$ inches in diameter. Wrap up the cylinder and put in the fridge to firm up. When ready to serve, slice into $1/2$-inch disks (or however much you want). It keeps for a few days, but you'll be using it at every opportunity.

Q: **This looks a little plain. No sauce?**

A: No. A good piece of well-marbled beef not only doesn't need sauce, it probably doesn't benefit from it—you're paying good money (in fact, *exorbitant* money) for this meat, and you want its flavor to shine through, not drenched in a creamy au poivre sauce; you might as well go for that cheap-ass London broil.

twice-baked potatoes with cheddar and caramelized onions

Let's face it: Baked potatoes are boring. And no matter what your topping, it's always going to seem like a you-didn't-try-very-hard dish. But with the simple addition of "Twice-Baked" and the remarkably easy process of caramelizing some onion, you transform the dish from Outback Steakhouse level to a side dish à la Morton's.

serves 2

2 large Yukon gold potatoes (about 1 pound)

4 tablespoons unsalted butter

2 tablespoons extra-virgin olive oil

2 medium Vidalia or yellow onions, halved and thinly sliced

3/4 cup grated sharp Cheddar cheese

1/4 cup whole milk

2 teaspoons salt, plus more to taste

1 teaspoon freshly ground black pepper, plus more to taste

1/4 cup minced chives

Preheat the oven to 400°F.

Prick the potatoes all over with a fork. Place them on a foil-lined baking sheet and cook for 1 hour, or until totally tender when pierced with the tip of a knife.

Meanwhile, prepare the onions: In the biggest skillet you have, melt 2 table-spoons of the butter with the olive oil over medium heat. Add the onion slices and cook, stirring frequently, for 5 minutes, until they take on just a little bit of color. Reduce the heat to very low and let cook for 30 to 40 min-utes, until a soothing golden color and a soft, *soft* consistency. Set aside.

Remove the cooked potatoes from the oven and reduce the temperature to 350°F. When the potatoes are cool enough to handle, halve lengthwise. Using a large spoon, scoop out most of the flesh, leaving behind a 1/4-inch-thick cup of potato skin. Set the cups aside.

Place the flesh in a medium mixing bowl. Add the remaining 2 table-spoons of butter, the cheese, milk, and the salt and pepper. Loosely mash with a fork or potato masher—you're not going for a thoroughly smooth purée here, just incorporating the flavorings. Taste, and add more salt and pepper if you think it needs it.

Mound the mashed potato mixture into the cups, and top with the caramelized onions. At this point, you can set them in the refrigerator, wrapped in foil, to finish baking later (or the next day). Or just continue on: Place the cups on the baking sheet and return them to the oven. Bake for 10 to 15 minutes (or 25 to 30 minutes, if they've chilled), until heated through. Allow to rest 5 minutes before serving. Top with a sprinkle of chives.

hot, garlicky swiss chard with almonds

Spinach is the customary rabbit food to serve with steak—sautéed spinach, creamed spinach, whatever spinach. Don't get me wrong: I love spinach, and this recipe works well with almost any sauté-able green. But how about we mix things up?

serves 2

2 pounds Swiss chard, stemmed, washed

2 tablespoons extra-virgin olive oil

2 teaspoons crushed red pepper flakes (1 teaspoon if your date is a wuss)

2 garlic cloves, thinly sliced

3/4 cup slivered almonds

1 teaspoon salt, plus more to taste

1/2 teaspoon freshly ground black pepper, plus more to taste

Bring a large pot of salted water to a boil. Add the chard and cook for 2 minutes, until wilted and tender. Drain in a colander, rinse with cold water, and allow to cool slightly. Using your hands, squeeze out as much of the water as possible. Pat dry with paper towels. Coarsely chop into large pieces and, again, pat dry with paper towels.

In a large skillet over medium flame, heat the olive oil. Add the pepper flakes and the garlic and sauté for 30 seconds, until fragrant. Add the chopped chard and slivered almonds and sauté, stirring once or twice, for 5 minutes; the chard should take on a little bit of brownness. Mix in the salt and pepper, taste, and add more if you want. Serve hot.

gooey chocolate-coffee brownie cake

This is not the dessert you fix for His Excellency the Honorable Ambassador of Norway. In fact, the word *gooey* rarely belongs on a formal menu. This is an easy, regular-guy dessert, and it is absolutely delicious—a chewy brownie floating on a warm chocolate pudding.

serves 4

1 1/4 cups granulated sugar

7 tablespoons cocoa powder

1 cup all-purpose flour

2 teaspoons baking powder

1/4 teaspoon salt

1/2 cup whole milk

1/3 cup unsalted butter, melted

1 1/2 teaspoons pure vanilla extract

1/2 cup light brown sugar

1 1/4 cups hot coffee

Vanilla ice cream, for serving

Mint leaves, for garnish

Preheat the oven to 350°F.

In medium bowl, combine 3/4 cup of the granulated sugar and 3 tablespoons of the cocoa with the flour, baking powder, and salt. Blend in the milk, butter, and vanilla; beat until smooth. Pour the batter into a glass or metal 8- or 9-inch square baking pan.

In small bowl, combine the remaining 1/2 cup granulated sugar and 4 tablespoons cocoa with the brown sugar. Sprinkle over the batter. Pour the hot coffee over the top. Do not stir.

Bake 35 to 40 minutes, until the center is set. (Test by inserting a toothpick or a knife; if it comes out clean, it's ready.) Let it cool a few minutes, then eat with lots of vanilla ice cream. Garnish with mint leaves.

straightguyFAQ

Q: Coffee paired with chocolate and sugar—for dessert? Just thinking about it will make me bounce off the walls all night. Are you crazy?

A: Easy, big fella: Decaf works fine.

feed her

It's all well and good to cook a complete three-course meal from scratch, but sometimes that's simply not practical. Or maybe you're just not the man for that particular job. Whatever the reason, you're not going to be whipping up the soufflé tonight. But that doesn't mean your home-dining options are limited to takeout beef lo mein or a pepperoni pizza. Today, even the most bare-bones supermarkets stock a tremendous variety of prepared, ready-to-eat (or nearly so) foods that, in the right combinations and the right presentations, can give you a no-brainer epicurean delight. And if you're lucky enough to live near a gourmet or specialty-foods store, your options expand exponentially.

As with the home-cooked meals on the previous pages, the main point here is just that you try.

faking it
no-cook dinners

Head to the fancy food shop—you know, the one where people are streaming out with baguettes poking out of their bags. Yes, this may be a little more expensive than the forty-two-aisle shopping-plaza supermarket. But you will walk out with what, for all intents and purposes, will be a delicious, home-cooked meal.

Look for whatever you think will taste the best. Does the market specialize in rotisserie chickens? By all means, score one of those. A good cheese counter? Excellent. Prewashed micro-greens? Bring it on. Whatever looks good, whatever the other customers are swarming around, that's what you want.

Rustic Chicken Dinner

This is your white T-shirt of suppers: Simple, yes, but it can also be cool or sophisticated, if pulled off with style. Here's what you'll need, and what to do:

Rotisserie chicken

Mixed prewashed salad greens, such as mesclun or baby spinach

Vinaigrette dressing

Country-style bread and high-quality imported butter

1. Keep that chicken hot—either in the container it came in (probably a foil-lined bag), or in a 225°F oven, or both.

2. A few minutes before it's time to eat, *lightly* dress the greens in a salad bowl. Slice the bread.

3. Unwrap the chicken, and quarter it. This will be easy to do—just jiggle a fork and knife around the major joints, and the thing will separate itself into four perfect serving sizes.

4. Mound some dressed greens in the center of each plate. Ask her whether she prefers breast or thigh. Place her serving and yours in the middle of the mound of greens, and, using a fork, sort of rub the chicken across the greens. The heat from the chicken will wilt the greens a bit—this doesn't mean it'll turn them soggy, which you'd do by overdressing them, but it just means that they'll warm up, sag, and soften a little. As you read this, you may not be thoroughly enticed. But trust me, this is good stuff.

5. Place a few slices of bread on each plate. Serve with the luscious European butter. Or good plates, please, with real silverware. Go the extra yard, and buy a couple of cloth napkins. Use them here.

Just Desserts

So you had an early dinner, then saw a movie or a show. It's ten o'clock, Saturday night. You'd like to get her back to your place. Here's what that "anything" should be: At dinner, when the waiter brings the dessert menu, say to her, "I hope you don't mind, but I put together some dessert for later. So should we skip this now?"

Back at the home front, you've cleaned the joint, dimmed the lights, and acquired:

A chocolate dessert Your choosing, from the best bakery you know. This can be a rich chocolate torte (fancy word for "cake"), a selection of chocolate truffles, a mousse, or anything else that catches your eye. Not candy, though, and nothing that comes shrink-wrapped.

Strawberries Rinse them, dry them with paper towels, then put them in the fridge, on a damp paper towel folded on a plate.

Champagne The good stuff. Piper-Heidsieck, Veuve, Mumm, Perrier-Jouet are some great options, all running about $35. Chill it. Locate your glasses, preferably classic flutes. If you don't have these, consider buying at least two of them, available almost anywhere glasses are sold, beginning at about $5. Make sure they're spotlessly clean.

So then, the show is over, you open your door, show her to the softly lit sofa, and say you'll be right back. Head into the kitchen, and emerge seconds later with your bottle of champers and two glasses. Wrap the bottle in a clean dishcloth or cloth napkin, which prevents it from slipping out of your hands, absorbs any overflow spillage, *and* makes you look cool, all at once. Remove the foil, and slowly, *gently* twist out the cork. It should not fly across the room, it should not explode like a backfiring Harley; those are rookie moves. It should make a soft pop and a slow hiss. Pour her a glass and hand it to her; pour yourself a glass and set it down. Say, again, "I'll be right back."

Plate your chocolate dessert, and arrange strawberries alongside. Emerge from the kitchen carrying your plate of brown-and-red treats, with clean silverware and clean cloth napkins. Place them in front of her. Pick up your champagne, clink glasses, and enjoy.

5 Ways to Dress Up a Salad

Good greens and a good dressing are all you need for a good salad, but here are some ways to raise good to great

1. Wild Mushroom Salad For an earthy indulgence. Wild mushrooms are available at good produce markets, farm stands, and an increasing number of supermarkets. In a small nonstick skillet, sauté a handful of stemmed and cleaned wild mushrooms (such as chanterelles, morels, shiitakes, portobellos, and creminis) in 1 tablespoon of olive oil until they soften, about 1 minute. Remove from the flame. Add 1/2 tablespoon of truffle oil, 1/4 tablespoon of white-wine vinegar, and a pinch of salt and pepper, and mix. Pour the mushrooms and their warm dressing over the greens, toss, and serve.

2. Salad with Goat Cheese Croutons Toast 6 slices of a baguette in a 300°F. oven for 10 minutes, until dried out and hard. Spread a tablespoon of soft goat cheese over each toast and return to the oven for 1 minute. Arrange the warm croutons over a lightly dressed salad, and crack some pepper over the top of everything.

3. Herb Salad with Herbed Vinaigrette Buy a few bunches of fresh, soft herbs—your choice, such as oregano, thyme, basil, sage, marjoram, parsley. Or even experiment with different varieties of these herbs—lemon thyme, say, or Thai basil. Remove the herb leaves from the stems. Finely chop enough of the leaves to total about 1/2 teaspoon of greenery, add this to your vinaigrette, and combine in a food processor or blender. Toss the other leaves, whole, with greens. And then toss the greens with the now-green dressing, serve, and wonder at how much flavor you've just added with so little effort.

4. Insalate di Antipasto At your fancy-food shop's deli counter or your friendly neighborhood salumeria (a type of Italian store that specializes in meats like salami; hence the name), buy small quantities—no more than a few ounces, or $1/2$ cup—of any (or all) of the following: marinated mushrooms; mixed pickled vegetables; roasted red bell peppers; artichoke hearts; marinated olives; prosciutto or other good ham; fontina or other sharp cheese; fresh mozzarella; anchovies or sardines. Clean one large head of romaine lettuce, separate the leaves, and form into a bed on a large platter. Drizzle with extra-virgin olive oil and vinegar, and add a dash or two of salt and freshly ground pepper. Then arrange each antipasto element into its own little mound, nicely separated from the others. Serve with a hearty semolina bread and a glass of Chianti.

5. Heirloom Tomato Salad In late summer, when heirloom tomatoes are in season, buy one or two of as many varieties, in as many different colors, as you can find. Note that heirloom tomatoes, unlike most other commercially available varieties, can be pretty unattractive: With mottled skin and strange shapes, they look like candidates for cosmetic surgery more than a beautiful meal. But as long as they're ripe to the touch, buy them. Once sliced, their shapes and mottled skin won't matter a bit. Arrange these slices of different colors, shapes, and sizes over a bed of the greens of your choice, dressed very lightly; you don't want to overwhelm the distinct tastes of the different tomatoes. Serve with a sprinkling of coarse sea salt and freshly ground pepper.

The Art of Tszujing Dinner
How to Dress a Plate

Think of that piece of parsley at Denny's—it's the Slam in the Grand Slam Breakfast, and all the difference between fast food and good food, fast. Well, not really. But even something as hackneyed as a sprig of parsley can make a difference. We're not trying to be pretentious or fussy here—just to make the food look its best. Here are some other hints to dress up your plate.

Parmesan shavings Instead of the sawdust consistency of grated cheese, use a vegetable peeler to shave off little curlicues to top pastas, risottos, or salads.

Herb shower If you used any herbs whatsoever in the cooking—or even if you didn't—mince another tablespoon's worth. Just before serving, shower these minced little green bits all over the plate. Especially dramatic against a white plate.

Angle the food Rather than setting a pork chop alongside a mound of mashed potatoes, try this: Mound the potatoes a little higher than you might think looks right; place one end of the pork chop on the middle of the potato mound. The chop will depress the mound a bit but will be propped up on an angle. A little height and angle can go a long way toward a professional-looking presentation. Just don't get carried away; "tall food" is *so* eighties.

Wear white There are all kinds of china and casual dinnerware on the market, some of which features beautiful hand-painting and intricate designs. But almost nothing is more flattering to the food itself—the main event, in my mind—than a plain, simple plate. A white plate. For much the same reason, wineglasses should always be clear and not tinted with color; the color of the wine itself is part of the pleasure

Clean the plate No matter how carefully you placed that coq au vin onto a plate, some sauce splattered across to the other side. Right before bringing the plate to the table—not five minutes before, but five seconds before—wipe the edge with a clean dishtowel.

"Life is busy. Why get worked up about a little thing called hygiene? One easy answer is: Women notice."

grooming

part 2

Why bother, right?

Maybe you've had a bad hair decade. And maybe your bathtub's got more rings around it than an old-growth redwood. But life is busy. Why get worked up about a little thing called hygiene? One easy answer is: Women notice. Hair, nails, skin, the wafting bouquet of your fuzzy parts—for whatever reason, women pick up on these details, and they care.

Neglect comes in many guises. Some men really do mean to take better care of themselves but just never get around to it. Or they don't have the know-how to try. A lot of guys I meet aren't trained to think about grooming at all, aren't self-aware about this. And by not self-aware, I'm talking about the kind of man who isn't aware that there are actual tufts of hair protruding from his nostrils. They walk around in their life—all the time, all day—living with this hair. And if they do notice it, they think, "Okay, well, that's just what my nose does. On *my* nose, hair comes out of the nostrils, and on Tom Cruise's nose, it doesn't; I guess that's why I'm not a movie star." Somehow it just never occurs to them that these little twigs can be easily hacked off. What if you made eye contact with some stunning girl from across the room? She walks over to you and she's got . . . full-on nose-bush. How would you feel? It would freak you out. Why do you think it doesn't freak women out when they see it on a man? It does.

Primping ain't easy, boys. It takes work. But the real trick is doing it not just for someone else (though being aware of how you come off in public isn't a bad thing), but for you. It's time now to take your hygienic well-being into your own hands. Repeat after me: I am an uncouth, untweezed, improperly exfoliated stink-bomb of a man who'd best clean up my act (and bathroom) before five gay guys have to break down my door, restock my medicine cabinet, and forcibly tousle my hair.

Good grooming isn't just about aesthetics. Looking hot is one goal—but looking good and feeling happy is a better one. This is just one more aspect of how we present ourselves to the world. How we dress, where we live, what we talk about—all that's about self-expression. Grooming is no different. For some reason, men have really missed out on an education in style. Whether it's clothing or knowing how to take care of your skin, your nails, or your teeth, in American culture these things have always been thought of as feminine topics. Why that is I have no idea. Puritan values? Disappointingly small migration of quality male manicurists to the Old West? Now, though, the role of a man is changing within a society that's changing. You could write a whole book on that. But the point is that guys, gay and straight, feel a certain freedom now to think about how they're taking care of themselves and how they're expressing themselves through their personal aesthetic. Not a minute too soon.

When I was about eight, I was on a playground and saw this older guy who had this feathered Shawn Cassidy cut. I was just a little kid, but I remember having this very clear, conscious grooming awakening, and I thought: I want that hairstyle! For me, the fascination with the hairstyle was its power to transform: It could transform me from something I wasn't too psyched about—an awkward kid, just like any other awkward kid—to something I felt better about. And felt more in control of.

Not everyone has a feathered-cut "aha!" moment on the way to self-knowledge, but we can all spend a few minutes a day trying to look and feel our best. Beyond good looks and good hygiene, the basic philosophical argument for better grooming is this: You owe it to yourself, you owe it to the universe—and, yes, you owe it to the Fab Five—to be the best possible human being you can be. Period. This involves a lot of subjects, big and small. I've tried many things—studied the healing arts, spent time in ashrams, learned yoga, and went to hair school—all important to who *I* am as a human being. But where I really find fulfillment is in teaching other people to look and be their best. That means top to bottom, inside and out. It means the things we do for ourselves—the little attention-to-detail things that nobody else will ever notice—and what we pluck for others.

Now let's get you cleaned up.

straightguyFAQ

Q: Can I buy gel at the supermarket?

A: Yes and no. Drugstores, beauty-supply shops, your local stylist, and even a well-stocked supermarket all carry a range of products, with the better stuff sold by the specialists.

Good-Grooming Checklist

Here's what you should have some-where in your bathroom (preferably in a well-organized medicine cabinet). The key elements—what you can't live without—are simple:

Facial cleanser—not a bar soap (see page 106)

Moisturizer with an SPF of 15 or higher (see page 108)

Exfoliating scrub to use once a week (see page 107)

Shampoo *and* conditioner—that is, not a two-for-one shampoo-with-conditioner

Hair product (see pages 92–95)

Razor, shaving cream, and (bonus) shaving brush (see pages 113–114)

Nail clippers—yes, you need to clip your nails, not just chew them (one for the fingers, a larger one for the toes)

Deodorant or antiperspirant

Pain relief of some sort, along with a first-aid kit

Mouthwash

Nose-hair trimmer (see page 98)

Comb or brush

And, it goes without saying (or it *should* go without saying, but I'll say it anyway):

Toilet paper. You can never have too much of it, and you can rest assured that if you run out of it, she will run out on you. And please, guys, spend a little more for the good stuff.

Toothbrush. If the bristles have disinte-grated to the texture of a fine down, or are discol-ored, or are falling out when you brush, get a new one. In fact, get a new one every month or so; it's just a toothbrush. Have extras, kept in their wrap-ping, for guests. Especially if you're single.

Toothpaste. Keep the cap on it, gents. There's very little more disgusting than dried, crusted-on toothpaste clogging the spout—ex-cept, perhaps, the idea that actual bacteria and maybe even bugs are crawling into the un-capped tube *as you read this.* Toothpastes with whitening agents are great.

Dental floss. I'm not your dentist, and I'm not going to lecture you on how important it is to care for your gums, and I'm not going to tell you to floss every day . . . well, I guess I am. Do it.

If you put in long hours at the office, it helps to have a little pick-me-up at some point in the day. Now that the three-martini lunch is out of style, try a little good hygiene instead: keep a Dopp kit in your desk with travel-size containers of mouthwash, facial cleanser, toothbrush and toothpaste, moisturizer, and maybe a little spray toner (a great way to hydrate midday, but perhaps a little advanced). When you hit that post-lunch fatigue, head to the men's room and freshen up.

hiptip

hair
the good, the bad, and the ugly

One of the reasons the straight guys on the show come around to the idea of better all-around man maintenance is they're faced with (and sometimes a little forced into) taking that plunge into something they wouldn't otherwise try on their own. For some in the stylist's chair, parting with their shag or that nine-year-old ponytail is as tough as killing a beloved pet. But they take a chance and end up happy with how they look and how they feel. Is it possible to get overly meticulous about your hair and get obsessive about products and be all creepy about it? You have a long way to go—but, yes, definitely. If there's no soul behind it, that shows, and it comes across as flat and deadening as hair spray. (Remember Bret Easton Ellis's protagonist in *American Psycho*? Well-groomed, yes, but not exactly a role model for your thinking, non-criminally-insane hetero.) It's not just about working on your style so you can strut out there and be a Cool Dude with Great Hair. It's about feeling good. And it's natural to feel better when you take care of yourself. Hair is the most visible thing we can play with to change our appearance, so start on top. It's crucial to find a stylist you trust—not only will they help you with a cool new haircut, they can also be a great source of expertise on how to style and care for it.

Product: A Hair-Care Lexicon

gel Goes on wet, stays looking wet. Some have very strong hold, though these tend to be thick and goopy. For fine hair in need of control, look for a light gel. The heavy-duty gels dry wet and set hard—very B&T (see Glossary), not nice to touch. If you think you need heavy gel, try a grooming cream instead. Apply to towel-dried hair (not too wet), working in thoroughly, then style. If your hair isn't very fine, after the gel dries you can add a light pomade for easy texture and shine.

grooming cream or paste Creamy or clear, from a tube or a canister. Before applying to dry or almost dry hair, rub it in your hands until it warms a bit (this is called emulsifying). Some are as light as lotion; others, a heavier paste. Great for curly or unruly hair, or straight hair with a textured cut—really, almost any hair except fine. Provides weight and separation and hold, but not as firm as a wax. Creams and pastes don't dry hard, which means a more natural look. Allows for texture and movement. The key is to consciously create a look—without looking like you tried too hard. Experiment with a cream and a paste, or talk to your stylist, to see which works best.

WITH PURE BOTANICAL ESSENTIALS
AVEC DES ESSENTIELS BOTANIQUES PURS
CON ESENCIAS BOTANICAS PURAS

ROSEMARY MINT

REJUVENATING STYLING GEL
GEL STYLISANT RAVIVANT
GEL ESTILIZANTE REJUVENECEDOR

AROMATHERAPY
AROMATHÉRAPIE
AROMATERAPIA

200 ml / 6.7 FL. Oz. (US)

gel

grooming CREME

the dream creme for those who love to look polished, elegant and smooth but hate to work at it.

crème de soins* est la crème rêvée pour ceux qui aiment avoir l'air soigné, élégant et poli mais détestent y passer du temps.

FL. OZ / OZ LIQ / 150 ml e

crea

wax Serious hold. Waxes are great for details—separating a single strand, roughing up a patch in the back. Generally heavy, a little bit of Elmer's glue for the head. Always use a water-soluble one. Good for people with thick and straight hair with a textured cut. If the hair has no texture in it and you add wax, it's going to hang there like a weight. If you prefer how your hair behaves the second or third day after shampooing, but you shampooed today and want that better feel, wax can help: Apply a light wax as a base to your dry hair, then re-wet your hair slightly and add a small amount of texturing cream.

hairspray Um, no. Pretty much never okay, unless you're working some advanced gel-wax-spray combination system with the quick spray at the end to hold the concoction together. (Or you have to take a picture and need to hold a look.) This is generally beyond the abilities of the styling amateur. We want malleable hair, and all you get with spray is stuck.

pomade More shine, less hold than a grooming cream. If your hair finish is too matte, it adds shape and texture as well as shine. Provides weight, though it's usually a bit oily. Won't dry hard—good hand feel—but it's not going to give as much in the way of separation and texture as a grooming cream. Good for all types except fine, oily hair. Always start with less than you think you'll need—you can always add more.

pomade

hairspray

hiptip

Be faithful to your stylist, but not to your shampoo. While it's great to find and stick with products that do us right, your hair will actually benefit from exposure to new products, ideally every 3 to 4 weeks. You'll get better results—and an excuse to go shopping around for the latest hair-care products.

Stylish Maneuvers

Mess with Your Head

Whatever your hair style, the key is to allow it to have movement and texture. What works for my hair won't necessarily work for yours. What our cuts should have in common is that a stylist worked the hair to its potential. Some haircuts require a tight, even finish, like balding guys who are wearing it short. For medium-length hair, though, it's generally preferable to add texture—the hair should be cut into; little bits cut from it will create texture. Then you need a product that can accentuate that depth. My hair is a little dry, a little poufy, just like most everyone else's hair. But with grooming paste (see page 93) and a little working over, I can create not only shape but great texture.

Experiment

I never put just one product in my hair. If I'm getting ready to go out, I'll usually put some kind of grooming paste or cream in, then I'll go back with something a little waxier that's just in my fingertips and that I can use to tszuj a little bit. As the hair is drying and starts looking a little matte, maybe I'll take a little pomade and work it in just to get that shine and moisture. Three or four products at a time is pretty advanced stuff, but have fun with it.

The Tao of the Tousle

For artfully unkempt hair, always work your grooming product in from the back of the head at the crown. It will save you from the very uncool look of having greased up everything but the blind spot on the dark side of your head.

nose-hair trimmer

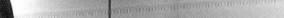

"Here's a crazy idea: battery-powered nose-hair trimmer. Stick it up there once a week. Bye-bye ugliness, hello evolved man. Dude, it's power tools for your nostrils!"

mowing
your lawns

If the hair on the top of your head is a canvas for glorious self-expression, the rest of your fuzz crop is best stifled and hidden away. What evil sprouts from the pits and pores of man! Most of what we talk about when we talk about good grooming has to do with getting in touch with the natural equilibrium of your body. But when it comes to unwanted body hair, the message is different: Practice manscaping. Think of it as a giant game of whack-a-mole: Your hairs keep coming up where they're not welcome, and your job is to weedwhack them into remission.

all aboard the monobrow—

Unruly eyebrows are rarely sexy. One long hedgerow of brow-bush is never the right answer. A lot of guys know this but don't think about a solution. If they have a beer belly, they know going to the gym can help. But with a lot of body-maintenence issues, they just don't have direction. When you say to them, "You know what, dude, you can tweeze those areas in between your eyebrows or have them waxed, and you can go in for some contouring so subtle that nobody will ever notice what's missing, and it will lift your eyes a little bit" . . . well, nobody's told them this before. Guys, listen up: You can look better for not a lot of effort.

If you are cursed with heavy foliage or conjoined caterpillars, you can approach the problem a number of ways: pluck (do not shave!) the unruly hairs yourself whenever they encroach on what should be a total demilitarized zone; or ask your stylist to give them a good trim to hold you to the next visit; or you can actually see an aesthetician (they work at spas) who can shape and separate your unibrow. A brow waxing costs $15 to $25, and should be done whenever you notice encroaching monobrow-ness. (With repeated waxing, the hair will eventually grow in thinner.) Just make an appointment at any spa. Remember: two eyes, two eyebrows!

straightguyFAQ

Q: What's the point of being a straight guy if I go and shave off all my manly hair?

A: Some body hair is hot and some is not. Nice chest hair can add definition to your body and be very sexy. But remove hair that's irregular or unpleasantly plush. Regular trimming will emphasize the manly attributes.

The Gentle Art of Manscaping

Think of it as a wilderness. In the beginning, there are trees and forests and wild weeds everywhere. And then civilization comes along and somebody says, I'm going to keep a garden. I'm going to separate these flowers from the rest. All of a sudden, rather than this unruly growth, you have a landscaped world.

In our case, body hair is the natural bounty, and what we need is a little manscaping. How you tend your garden will depend on what you've got growing and how much you (or your girlfriend) prefer a smooth playing field. In any case, the goal is management, not total removal. Unless you're doing shirtless combat with Jackie Chan or racing the Tour de France next year, you don't need to shave it all off. What you don't want is ugly tufts of hair on view, creeping up the back of your neck, or poking out of shirt necklines and short sleeves.

Back hair is where we see the most egregious overgrowths. Mow your backyard, people! How you do this depends on both the seriousness of the problem and your commitment to tackling it.

shaving Unless you've got just a patch of peach fuzz on a reachable bit of your back, this is not where you want to experiment with do-it-yourself solutions. Plus it's hard to properly lather up your lats. So all in all, not really the solution.

waxing Quick, easy, and it works. Not permanent, but it lasts three to four weeks. Does it hurt? Of course. But do you know what she goes through for you?

electrolysis Permanent, expensive, and kind of weird. But if you've got a moderate mess to deal with and have the spare time and funds to have it obliterated, this could be the right way to go.

laser hair removal Expensive and somewhat painful, but permanent. Could be the right solution for you. Not a casual thing, though: Consult your dermatologist for advice.

Advanced Manscaping
The Hair Down There

Problem pubes. It happens. You can control it. Women go to great lengths to control it, and you are a happier straight man for it. You knew this, right? For the most part, women trim it, they wax it, they do crazy things with strange names so that they can wear very, very tiny thongs.

So—and I know this is touchy territory—if guys have freakishly long fluffy man bush, then they should just apply a little manscaping. Clean it up. This works on a case-by-case basis, and it's hard for me to make a precise prescription, but a lot of guys would do well for themselves if they trimmed. First of all, shorter hair makes everything around it look bigger (you know what I'm talking about). Second, it's more attractive to women. You needn't go nude, and you shouldn't get *too* close. Use an electric shaver with a protective grill and go easy. The point isn't to draw attention to your workmanship ("Hey, great crotch cut!"), but to subtly reshape the testicular topiary for a cleaner, more presentable package.

skin secrets

that every woman knows—and you should too

Your skin is your armor and also your weakest link. Nothing else is as vulnerable to life's elements, and yet nothing is as easily ignored by men as the health and well-being of the skin they're in. Treat your skin well—give it the cleansing, the nutrients, and the pampering it needs—and it will pay you back by looking radiant, young, and healthy. Let the gunk build up as it does on some of your bathtubs, and your skin will look every bit as grim and glum.

Have you ever noticed your typical American woman's arsenal of skin-care products? I'm not talking about lipstick, eyeliner, and other purely feminine articles; I'm talking about their lotions and potions, their creams and gels, their little tubes of this and jars of that. All those products maintain healthy skin or solve skin problems. And none of these problems is unique to the female anatomy. They're problems that men also face; we just aren't accustomed to solving them.

We should be. The difference between healthy and unhealthy skin isn't subtle; it's dramatic. And it can make all the difference between looking good and looking ghoulish.

If you're looking for an astringent (which contracts your pores, keeping unsightly secretions, especially excess oils, to a minimum) to clean your face, try witch hazel. It's natural, fragrance-free, and available for next to nothing at any drugstore.

hiptip

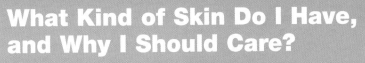

What Kind of Skin Do I Have, and Why I Should Care?

The four different skin types have their own problems and solutions—not every product or regimen is right for every skin. Find yours below, and find product explanations on the following pages.

Normal
This is the skin you have if you don't notice any particular issues. **problems:** You may have some slightly dry skin in places, slightly oily in others. **prevention:** You just need simple care and maintenance with a good cleanser (usually a foaming one), toner, and a straightforward moisturizer with antioxidant protection.

Oily
Big, open pores. Trouble in the T-zone (that greasy gulch between your brows, nose, and chin). **problems:** "Hey, I'm a zit! Get it?" Sadly, you get lots of it: whiteheads, blackheads, and general pore congestion. **prevention:** You need to use foaming cleanser, toner, and oil-free moisturizer.

Dry
Excessive, maybe even physically uncomfortable, tightness and dryness. **problems:** Signs of premature aging, including lines and wrinkles. **prevention:** Use a gentle cleanser—try a cream cleanser. For very dry skin, cleanse at night only; in the morning, just rinse with water. Try a rich moisturizing cream instead of a lighter lotion.

Combination
The combo platter. Dude, you need to pay attention. **problems:** The downsides of both dry and oily skin. **prevention:** First of all, use a gentle cleanser, preferably a foaming one. Then treat the dry areas only—not the oily ones, which are probably in your T-zone—with a cream moisturizer if your skin is *very* dry, or a lotion if mildly dry.

the daily regimen

Facial Cleanser

What so many men are missing is skin-care defense of any kind. They'll wash their face with the same bar of soap that they wash their ass with. That's not in any way a pleasant thought, but particularly troubling to me is the fact that regular bar soap is far too harsh for your face. You need a gentle cleaner (no fragrance, no detergent) that's specifically designed for the skin on your face. There are detergents in bar soap that can damage your face, that dry it out and lead to irrritation. Fragrances can also be a problem. Look for a cleanser that's made for the face and free of fragrances, detergents, and soaps, but instead includes sodium laureth sulfate. Also avoid cold creams, which contain irritants. A good cleanser will foam and wash away dirt without taking the face's natural and necessary oils with it. Use your cleanser twice a day: in the a.m., before shaving, and in the p.m., before sleeping. Look for skin-care products at a dermatologist's office, a spa, or upscale department stores. Foaming cleansers are more clarifying—they remove more oil, which is good for oily skin. (Not a surprise.) Cream cleansers do not foam and remove less—really, they just get rid of dirt; these are good for dry skin.

Q: **What can I do about oily skin?**

A: Try a skin toner, which is a mild, non-alcohol-based astringent. It can help close unsightly large pores, and remove residues that your cleanser couldn't clean up. It's especially useful for oily skin. And you should switch to an oil-free moisturizer.

straightguyFAQ

Exfoliants

Guys are generally not conversant with the language of exfoliation, which is the essential process of removing the superficial layer of dead skin cells. Unless your skin is freakishly perfect, you're going to get a build-up of dead skin cells on the surface of your skin. Not only does this make your skin look dull and lifeless, but it will prevent useful external nutrients from getting into the skin. Get an exfoliating scrub and use it at least once a week. A very fine grain is best for the face, and nonabrasive formulas are available if your skin is particularly sensitive. But do not use a body scrub on your face; it is too abrasive for delicate skin. And *any* exfoliant is going to be too abrasive for the area immediately surrounding your eyes—no exfoliating there, please.

Once you start using an exfoliant regularly, your face is going to look more vibrant, have that glow to it, but it's also going to allow the nutrients in your moisturizer to penetrate to the deeper layers of your skin. As a side note, exfoliation also helps prevent ingrown hairs and razor burn. Exfoliated skin makes shaving that much more pleasant.

Free Radicals

"Free radicals" may sound like a slogan on a bumper sticker, but what they should be is a rallying call for better skin care. Basically, a free radical is an atom that's lost an electron and tries to balance itself by stealing electrons from other cells. Whatever that means on a particle-physics level, what's important for your skin is that too many free radicals lead to a host of damaging effects, including the very visible signs of aging. The bad news is they come from things we can't avoid (like the environment and simply breathing) and all sorts of things a lot of people like to do (lying in the sun, smoking, drinking alcohol). The good news is that free radicals can be fought off with antioxidants, which come from various sources, including vitamins E and C (found in fruits). Eating well and taking supplements are solid ways to counteract free radicals and care for your skin. Vitamins A, C, and E are great, either applied topically or ingested (or, ideally, both). If your diet isn't particularly healthful, definitely take a vitamin supplement and find a moisturizer with both antioxidants and an SPF of 15 for greater protection.

Moisturizer

Most often, the best way to administer antioxidants (see above) to your skin is with a moisturizer, the most important element in preventing the signs of aging. Look for a moisturizer that's free of fragrance and hypoallergenic if you have sensitive skin that's easily irritated. Lotion is the most common form of moisturizer, good for normal or combination skin. Cream, which has more emollients, is best for very dry skin or for normal skin during the dry winter months. Oil-free moisturizer is for oily skin only.

"Your skin is your armor and also your weakest link. Nothing else is as vulnerable to life's elements, and yet nothing is as easily ignored by men."

moisturizer

To Do Today #1

The time to care for you skin is now—not later. Familiarize yourself with cleansers and moisturizers, or you'll soon wish you had. Here are the basics:

Cleanser is essential. It removes a day's worth of dirt and grime from your innoccent epidermus. Wash your face at least twice a day (morning and night) if you have normal or oily skin. If your skin is prone to dry out, just use the cleanser at night and rinse your face with plain old hot water in the morning.

Moisturizer sounds pretty girly, I know, but your skin will thank you. Any man who has made it past the oily-skin years of adolescence needs to be moisturizing his face. That goes double during the winter months, when the air is so much drier. If you are starting to see wrinkles, moisturizers will help to reduce the fine lines because your skin will be receiving essential emollients (a fancy word for good oils) and moisture. And prevention is the key here, guys: Start moisturizing today, *before* you think you need to, to prevent premature aging. A good moisturizer should have antioxidant cream and an SPF of at least 15.

Eat It—and Drink It

Moisturizer can only do so much. For a long-term investment in healthy skin, improve your diet; your skin will improve with it. Most of us run around nearly dehydrated a lot of the time. The rule about drinking 8 to 10 glasses of water every day is so, *so* essential. Just add water to your diet and you'll see better skin in days. And if you're drinking alcohol, you need to have even more water. Indulging in coffee, tea, or cola soft drinks? Drink even more water. Keeping hydrated internally is crucial to proper cellular activity in the skin.

Eating fish that's rich in omega-3 fatty acids helps improve skin tone—salmon in particular is a great skin-enhancing fish. In addition, snack on all those foods rich in vitamins E and A: carrots, nuts, spinach, avocado, and sunflower seeds. Not exactly buffalo wings and T-bones, I know. But they'll make you look better.

straightguyFAQ

Q: Okay, you got me to buy a moisturizer. When should I use it?

A: Twice a day is optimal. Moisturize *after* you shave, and then again after washing your face at night.

You Are My Sunshine—*Not*

The sun presents one of the greatest challenges to skin well-being. On the other hand, we can't totally avoid sunlight and be healthy, too. Luckily, sunscreens have graduated from tanning afterthoughts to a major component in a wide array of products, from lip balm to moisturizers. SPF, or Sun Protection Factor, is a rating meant to gauge the time you can wear the product in the sun before burning. For everyday products, start at SPF15. For intense sunning, find a higher number that works for you based on your complexion. Look for products that are free of lanolin, which is an irritant and too heavy.

As for getting a golden brown hue, leave out the sun altogether and try spray-on tanning at a salon. Not only is it realistic and completely safe, the airbrushed shading can actually contour the body, giving it the illusion of a fitter, more muscular you. (Hey, every bit helps.) If you're not that committed, a little at-home self-tanner can do a fine trick. Just be sure to follow the package directions, and apply the cream thinly and evenly. Having no tan is better than having a streaky tan. And be sure to wash your hands when you're done applying the product—tan palms just aren't a natural look.

The reason to go with the no-sun tan, as you probably know, is that the sun is dangerous. Any sun exposure, and especially burning, increases the long-term risk of skin cancer. More immediately, sun exposure greatly increases free-radical damage, leading to premature wrinkles, sun spots, and uneven skin tone.

If you already have sun-damaged skin, use moisturizers with antioxidants and an SPF of 30 (or higher). See a dermatologist for product and treatment recommendations. Sometimes they'll recommend a chemical peel or a long-term alpha/beta-hydroxy-acid treatment, via products, which will promote cellular rejuvenation and may reverse the signs of aging.

how to shave

Guys who complain about having to shave every day just aren't doing it right. Maybe you consider it a drag because that's what you do—drag your rusty razor across your poorly prepared face, leaving damaged skin and bloodied tissues in your wake. Think of shaving as a ritual, one that's all about being a man. A private time to ready yourself to face the day. An excuse to soothe your face with balms and swaddle it in steaming hot towels and chisel out a better face. Learn how to do it right and you'll look forward to the daily trim.

straightguyFAQ

Q: Are you tolling me I shouldn't use an electric razor?

A: A proper wet shave is much gentler on your skin than an electric shave—this may be counterintuitive, since the blade looks harsh and the electric head looks gentle. But trust me on this—wet shaves with traditional manual razors are the way to go. However, if you must, try to use one of the new electric shavers that you can get wet (water is one of the keys to a comfortable shave), and try to use it in the shower.

five elements of a perfect shave

The Prep

Hot, wet action is what you're after (as ever). But don't just slap some water from the sink across your cheeks and start scraping. Shaving takes time. It's a process—one that's better left unrushed. Start with a warm shower. (You can shower *while* you shave, but why combine two of the most private, reflective periods of your day?) The heat and moisture of the shower will soften your beard and open your hair follicles, allowing your stubble to be removed easily, comfortably, and with less risk of injury. The ideal shaving time is directly after you towel off. If you're on a shower strike (although, why would you be?), a warm compress—a wash-cloth that you've dampened with hot water—against the skin will work in its place. Next, as with any good grooming exercise, there are products to consider.

A lot of brands have gotten hip to preshave oils, which you apply to your skin before you lather up and shave. These soften the beard and provide lubrication—think of it as the KY Jelly of the shaving tango. Try a couple products to see which works best for you and your skin. (Men with oily skin may find some preshave oils overly oozy.)

The Lather

Preshave products are a bonus, not a necessity. But a great shaving cream is. What does a great shaving cream deliver? It will be thick and emollient. Just the word *emollient* gets me in a lather. The great shaving cream will not appear to be made of air. It will form a thick foam when it's rubbed into your beard. If it's thick and richly creamy, you can feel it going right up onto the skin and protecting it—it's wrapping the hair follicle in its creaminess. I myself am not a shaving-gel man, but some guys prefer gels to creams. Go your own way, but make sure you get emollient. Work it into your skin and don't rush it. There are moisturizers in there; let them do their job. You'll know it when you feel it.

The Blade

In the end, all razors are disposable, just like all toilet paper is disposable. That doesn't mean you go and buy the cheapest brand that proudly advertises, "Toss me, I'm useless!" The only thing those cheapie disposable razors have going for them is truth in packaging: Throw them out before you even use them. I wouldn't use them on my nose hair (not that I have nose hair). Get a razor that has a movable head and at least two blades. But even the fancy blades aren't going to last forever—in fact, if you have a coarse beard and shave every day, they shouldn't last until next week. I use one a week, but the exact number of uses you'll get out of a particular blade will depend on how well it's made and the strength of your facial hair. If you feel any drag at all when you shave—if you can feel it pulling the hairs and not cutting through them—throw the blade out and use a new one. Your face is not disposable.

The Technique

Okay, relax. Take a breath (but don't breathe in the foam). You've come this far. Your skin is buttered up. The stiff resolve of your follicles is beginning to wither. Too many guys are in a rush to the end here, speed-shaving around their features with demolition-derby results. (As with sex, faster is almost never better.) Remember, this is a ritual, a ceremony: Swift, easy, natural strokes are what you want. (Again, think sex.) Don't apply too much pressure while you go, pushing the blade into your cheeks—it's a ritual, but not a bloodletting. (And yet again . . .)

Follow the natural grain of your face. For most guys, this means shaving "down." When you go up, against the grain of your hairs, you tend to push up the follicle and drag it with the razor, irritating it and possibly leading to razor bumps and ingrown hairs. Dip your razor in warm water between strokes to unclog hairs and to warm it again for smoother cutting. If there are still patches of resistance, shave *across* the grain.

The After Party

Splash your face with cold water to refresh and close down the pores. Notice I said "splash" and not "smack upside." Similarly, splash and work into your skin an aftershave. Contrary to what your father may have told you, aftershaves should not burn like lye. And they shouldn't be composed entirely of scented alcohol. The purpose behind the highly alcoholic aftershaves in old-fashioned barbershops was to sterilize your skin after it had been in contact with what was pretty much a communal razor blade, to prevent disease from spreading. Since you're not sharing your razor with the rest of the neighborhood or any tubercular cousins, this sterilization shouldn't be your primary concern. So skip the high-alcohol-content ones, which will dry out and irritate your skin. Instead, go for a balm or gel made with natural or essential oils; I personally prefer a balm with shea butter. And be sure to try it out before shelling out—you might be allergic or just sensitive to some ingredients, and that's best learned while your cash is still in your wallet.

Q: What can I do about this one patch of upper neck that's always impossible to shave?

A: We all have parts that are harder to shave than others (for the really hard parts, see the section on manscaping). The trick here is to leave the problem area for last. That will give it the longest time to soften up under the lather, and give you a better chance of taking care of it.

the well-groomed man

5 grooming treatments to try before you're 35

Facial

There's something to be said for a woman's touch—and you'll be pleasantly surprised by just how violent and corrective these can be. Facials are great for cleansing, exfoliation, and extractions (that is, removing pore buildup with manual manipulations). Get a facial every six weeks or so—there are lots of gender-neutral spas for it. And it's a great opportunity to get product recon from an aesthetician.

---

hiptip

Straight-razor shaves from a barber are a treat, but not something you can do every day. One lesson to take home from the experience is the way he'll place a finger on one part of your face to create a little tension on the skin while he's shaving. The flatter the surface, the smoother the blade will cross it, the closer the shave. Try it. But without the horror-flick implement—straight razors are definitely *not* for home-schooled amateurs.

Manicure/Pedicure

Why not look good right down to your extremities? These treatments aren't about painted nails and foot massages (not that there's anything wrong with those). This is about tszujing your feet for sandal season and making something presentable out of your bitten fingernails.

Body Wax

Oh, come on. Women do it for you; return the favor. A couple seconds of pain. A new, smooth, less-revolting you—still you, but without the excess fur. Get it done at a spa. The cost is proportional to the area being treated.

Straight-Razor Shave

Hot towels! Blades to the jugular! And if you're lucky, a nose-hair clipping by a complete stranger.

A Proper Haircut

If you've spent three decades at the local barbershop, give a salon a try, if for no other reason than you will likely be surrounded by women touching each other, instead of by old men and Barbicide.

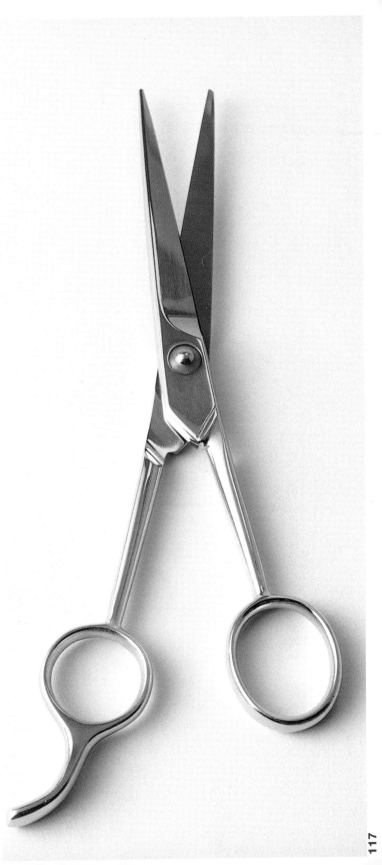

"My apartment shouldn't look like your apartment, and your apartment shouldn't look like Carson's (unless you're really, really into horses, which would be okay; we could work with that)."

decorating

Interior designers can be a little intimidating. It's not just our impeccable taste or the arsenal of fabric swatches we carry around, or even our uncanny ability to locate a diamond in the residential rough (or at least a futon hidden somewhere under a pile of laundry). Unlike the other guys, I'm not going through your underwear drawer or messing up your hair. But I am inside your lair, checking up on the way you live. What you sleep on. What "art" you have on the walls. What touching/disturbing childish night-light you keep in the bathroom. I'm in your place, critiquing your *stuff*. It gets personal. But I'm a professional, and I'm here to help.

I'm not the type of decorator to drop off some pretty furniture and speed away. What I like about my work is talking to clients about how they use their home, how they'd like to live in it, and what their tastes and enthusiasm amount to. That ongoing dialogue helps them express what they want and helps me visualize it. It would never make sense for me to barge into somebody's home and tell them exactly what fixtures and furniture and fabrics I think they need—one person's favorite color is the flash someone else sees in their really horrible, creepy nightmares. And I can't know that just by looking at a floor plan.

First of all, I don't have to live there. I don't want to; I've got my own place, thank you. But you *do* have to live there—not just sleep there, but *live* there, in *your* space. I hate to talk about "mistakes" in design choices, but if there's one mistake people make the most, it's not thinking in terms of personalizing their space. My apartment shouldn't look like your apartment, and your apartment shouldn't look like Carson's (unless you're really, really into horses, which would be okay; we could work with that).

The problem for most people is that there's nobody there to start that dialogue. I grew up in a house where design was spoken—loudly, in the case of my bedroom. The rest of the house was pretty traditional, but my room was tricked out in bright orange shag carpet, striped walls, mesh curtains, and an acid-green bedspread. I thought about these things a lot, and now I think about living spaces all the time. But for a lot of people, furnishing their house or apartment is just a matter of functional necessity: The coffee table broke, time to get a new coffee table. Which is too bad. Because thinking through your surroundings can be rewarding and fun, and you might realize that maybe you don't need a coffee table there; maybe there's something else that would work better in that space. Whatever I suggest for your home, you've got to be the one who's comfortable there. You should never be uncomfortable—from either the daintiness or the grime.

What I hope you can get is some inspiration to think about your own spaces. A lot of guys tell me they have no idea about interior design and can't identify what they like or don't like. But you get people talking about things they do know about—their work or what they collect, whatever—and you start to get at how they live and what they'd like their place to be like. A lot of guys—a lot of *people*—say they don't know anything about design. So I ask them what they *do* know about. If the answer is they like cars, I'll ask about their favorites, what model and year, which color with what interior they're into. And all of a sudden we're talking about color palettes and texture and design with a guy who "doesn't know anything about design." But now we're talking about design in a language he's comfortable with, reflecting a truer sense of who he is.

Hiring a designer to make chatty house calls—let alone totally make over your pad—is a luxury or a curse most people don't have the means or the time for. But anyone who's interested can spend a few hours thinking about how to better personalize his living quarters. One quick exercise is to take a better look at what you already own. Pick five favorite things from around the house. Could be anything—a picture frame, a souvenir, or a ceramic vase you picked up at a garage sale.

Then chose five favorite articles of clothing. Whatever they are, I guarantee you that when you lay these things out, a lot of information about you will come through. Use the objects to help you begin to cultivate your sense of style and interests, and the clothing as a springboard to help determine your color palette.

I'm not suggesting that you immediately retool your entire home around a couple of your favorite trinkets. The hardest part of any design project is getting started. So let's do that.

"Pick five favorite things from around the house. Could be anything—a picture frame, a souvenir, or a ceramic vase you picked up at a garage sale."

design
is a process
it's a studio apartment, not a château in provence

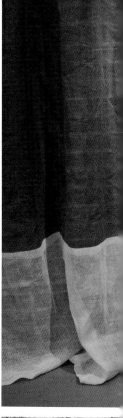

The first step you need to take is to understand your space. Ask yourself, What do I live in? Where the hell am I? Is this an A-frame with beamed ceilings or a post-war, Sheetrocked-within-an-inch-of-its-life starter apartment? The answer may sound obvious—you know where you live, or at least have a pretty good idea how to get there—but you'd be surprised how many people are living in denial about their surroundings. If you own a cozy little cottage on a hill, it just doesn't make sense to go for that SoHo loft look. Which is not to say that you're stuck with the particular personality of the space you inherited—you can change every single detail to fit your taste and crazy desire. But the first step to doing that—and to understanding what it is you actually plan to do—is to be honest about the factual, structural situation you're living in. We call this understanding the "bones" of your architecture.

Think about your own body. When you go shopping for clothes, your body is your architecture. And if you didn't know your own shape and frame, you might pick out things that don't work. Once you understand the basic framework, you can go about adapting that to your personal style. Most people say to me, "Thom, I really want to redecorate." Well, that's great. But we can't have that conversation until you tell me what it is we're working on. There's a lot of direction, inspiration, and important information that come from just recognizing the shape, type, and period of the architecture you're dealing with. You live in a renovated warehouse,

so you've given some thought to the height of your walls. When you're out buying a sofa and someone show's you a teeny, tiny little modern bench of a sofa with low back and arms, you can think, well, this is going to be dwarfed by those walls. Knowing the structural situation of your house is going to help you make decisions—and save money—along the way.

A lot of guys have no concept of this. They just say, "I want my house to be better looking." Take the time to understand your space, and you'll be ahead of the game. Even if it's a one-room apartment with a dumpster view, take an inventory of what's around you. This can be as simple as sitting in your room for five minutes. Look around and come up with your own concept of what the place is. Or you can delve deeper. Go to a bookstore and get a book about ranch houses if you live in one. Even the smallest amount of information gathering is like a missing link in the design process. Where are your windows? What's the shape of the room? What are the floors made of? What color is that dumpster?

left: When I was decorating our Queer Eye loft, people asked me how I was going to cover up all the pipes. Cover them up? Exposed pipes are the very essence of a New York loft, the inner workings of a place built for manufacturing. The walls are steeped in history and character, and I loved the challenge of transforming the space without sacrificing all the rich and distinctive qualities found there.

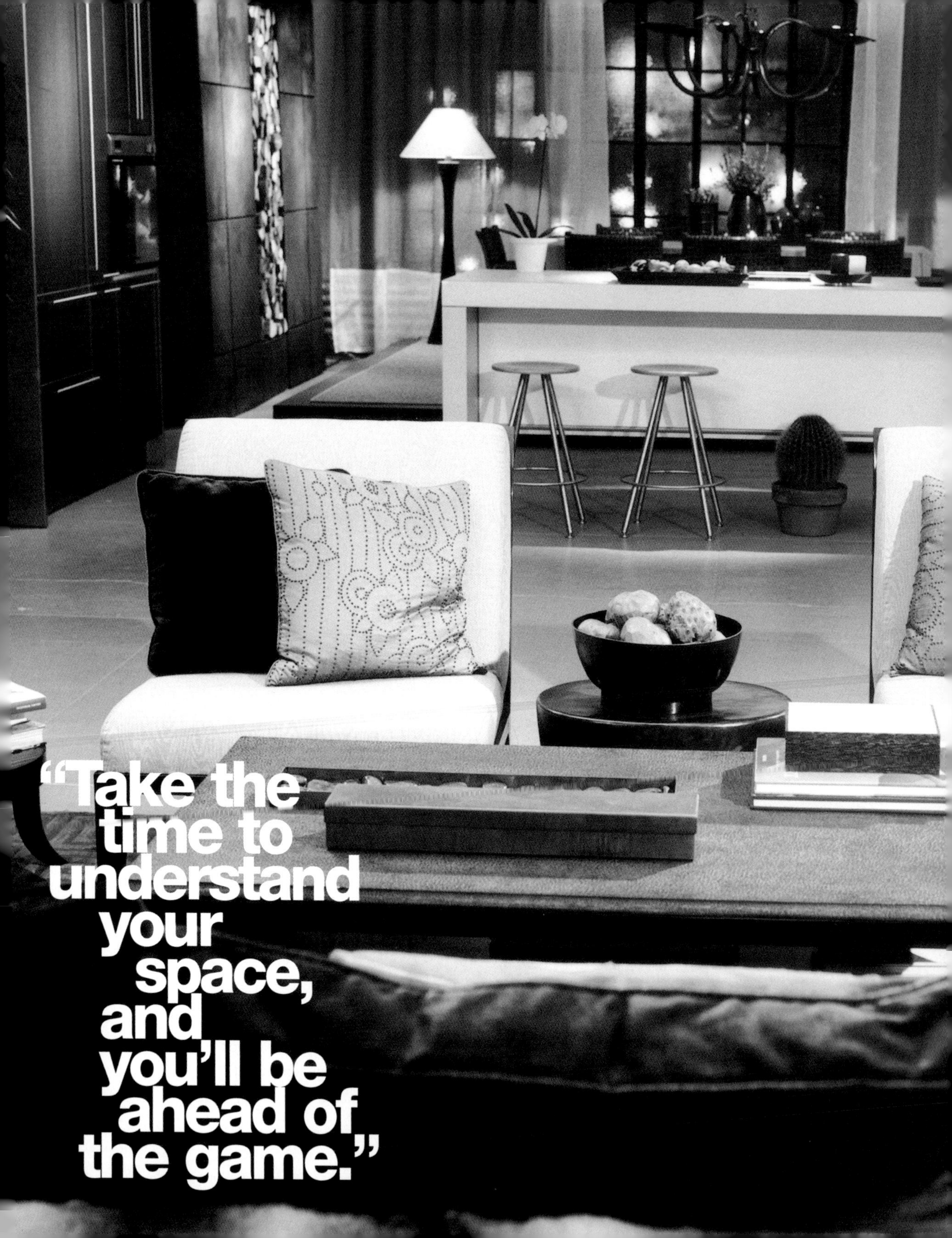

"Take the
time to
understand
your
space,
and
you'll be
ahead of
the game."

Flowing Through Space

When we found our loft, it was a pretty bleak, underdeveloped place. Someone had just plopped a kitchen down in one spot and dropped a sofa in another. All the furniture arrangements were coming off one side, so it felt exactly like a railroad apartment. You should always think about the flow of a space. Don't just press everything you own up against the wall and call it a room. Create spaces that people can walk through. Use furniture to break up and reframe awkward spaces.

left: To understand a loft, you have to realize that you've got one room, and you need to define areas within the space. I thought long and hard about how we'd be using our loft and what we would need out of it, and I planned the layout accordingly—a place for the Fab 5 to monitor the straight guys' progress on TV (foreground), a kitchen that isn't shut off from the action or shunted off to the side (middle ground), and a dining room to showcase Ted's skills (rear). Because it's a loft and we wanted to stay true to its roots, our look is simple and serene with pops of color and pattern. Many of the surfaces are natural—bronze panels, polished concrete, and exposed brick walls. The painted walls are done in light tones that won't compete with the heavy materials. Color is brought in through rugs, pillows, objects, and contemporary art.

"If you have the luxury of having a couple of rooms to live in, then you should come up with interesting ways to make them inviting."

I sleep fourteen hours a day and haven't eaten at my dining table since the early eighties . . .

Think about how you use your space. We all live in apartments or houses where many of the decisions—where to put what—are predetermined by convention. Electrical outlets are put in certain places. Hanging fixtures are in certain places. The dining room table goes here because . . . well, because that's where the dining room table has always gone. People will follow this blueprint, and it doesn't matter if they eat out every night of the week, they'll put a dining table in the center room of their house because they think they have to. And then they'll completely ignore it. They'll have a whole dining room setup and it's a completely unused part of the house.

People who haven't done any decorating—people renting an apartment, or just starting off in their first place—haven't thought about how they actually live in a place. They just inherit the space as is and throw their stuff into it. Which is fine. You can change that when you're ready. But what's more surprising to me is a lot of people who *have* decorated their homes based on an ideal that has nothing to do with who they are. It's not personal to them at all. I feel pretty strongly that if you have the luxury of having a

couple of rooms to live in, then you should come up with interesting ways to make them inviting. Living rooms should be lived in. The good china, if you have it, should be eaten off of. Here again, stopping and thinking about something we tend to take for granted is a great way to get moving on making your home a better place. When you sit up in bed, are you looking at a bathroom toilet, or are you looking out the window? We're not talking about high-concept feng shui here. Just a simple appreciation of what you do in your place and how it works. Take a few minutes to observe how you live in your home. If your living room is unlived in and you spend all your time at a computer in an office that's the size of a broom closet, take note.

left: Anything that reflects a personal interest will help make your place truly yours, whether it's framed photos, that collection of dead birds, or antique masks or shields.

... but I wouldn't mind
installing a jacuzzi in the den

Once you've evaluated what it is you do in your castle, think about what you'd *like* to do there. If all you do is play video games and eat potato chips—hey, we can make it work. You don't cook much, so we'll save our money on renovations in the kitchen and put the cash toward really comfortable chairs, or some very cool cushions or beanbags by the TV, something low to the floor to accommodate a number of friends, and at the best angle for playing. It's not about radically rethinking architecture, it's about rationally rethinking how you use it. It's about coming up with ways that people can really use the space as they need to—or as they want to.

Knowing where you're coming from and where you'd like to go is key to getting things right and also, just as important, to having the confidence to make decisions. The options out there for what you can buy are just mind-boggling. There are so many directions to go in, so much confusion, that you want to feel like you're not just making random decisions you'll regret later. So when you're standing in a store and looking at a chair, you're not just saying, "Hey, that's a cool chair." You're saying, "That chair has a nice high back that would look fantastic with the scale of my living room." Know your space and consider its uses and possibilities: This will give you a great plan of attack for whatever you're doing, from buying a new sofa to undertaking a massive redesign.

right: If wine is your thing, don't hide the bottles in the clammiest closet you can find. Go for it: Your passions should dictate your décor.

"Once you've evaluated what it is you do in your castle, think about what you'd *like* to do there."

straightguyFAQ

Q: My kitchen's boring and ugly—anything I can do short of spending thousands on remodeling?

A: Buying **new drawer pulls** and knobs for all your cabinets is an inexpensive, easy way to give an old kitchen a fresh look. So is doing the dishes.

A: Go window-shopping—wherever furniture is sold, just walk around and browse. (You don't need to stay on the *outside* of the window, by the way—it's still window-shopping if you're actually in the store but not intending to remove your wallet from your pocket.) Whether at the strip mall, an upscale national retailer, or temples of high-end Italian furniture, you need to know what's out there. And don't be afraid to talk to the in-store design professionals.

Before You Start: Make a Checklist

Before you commence tearing out every wall in your house or whimsically invest in a seventeenth-century faux-bamboo commode for your one-bedroom apartment, look around, take inventory, and make a list.

Measure your space. Don't obsess about every inch, but get a rough picture of the place so when you're out shopping you have an idea about what you're working with. How high are the ceilings? How wide are the doorways? What are the dimensions of the rooms you're decorating? Where are the windows placed?

If you have an elevator in your apartment building, find out what the biggest piece you can put in it is. If you have an elevator in your house, call me.

Same for all the stairwells. You don't have to be an interior decorator to know that if you're having a grand piano delivered to your fifth-floor walk-up and your stairs are two feet wide, you're out of luck.

Write down what you want to do in a particular room and what you'll need there that's missing. Plan to add a home office in that spare broom closet? Maybe take a look at your dining room instead—if you never eat there, wouldn't it be a great space for working?

thought

The TV Challenge

It's time for television to come out of the closet (what we at Queer Eye are all about!). I see too many people hiding their televisions and stereos in these big ugly cabinets and armoires. I would much rather see an attractive low cabinet with a TV resting on it. What's the point of hiding the stuff away inside something enormous and hideous? It's like the elephant in the room that everyone knows is there but nobody says anything about. If you're that ashamed, spend your money on a better-looking TV.

reality

hiptip

Architects make perspective drawings that are really just exercises in planning. You can do the same thing at home, even if drawing is not your forte. It will get you thinking in terms of spatial design. The more planning you do, the better. Let's say you are redecorating your bedroom. It's really important that you draw out the room and measure it. Figure out if a king-size bed fits in the room or if you have to go with a queen. (No puns, please.) If you're putting in bunks, how high are the ceilings? What wall makes the most sense for the bed to be up against, and what do you have to walk through on a midnight trip to the john? The more you war-game these things, the smarter your decisions will be.

work with your space, not against It

Here's some sage advice from someone who's struggled with some interesting spaces: Don't try to fight the place you're in or try to make it something that it's not. You'll end up putting most of your effort (and not a little of your money) into the fight, instead of into what you want your home to actually be. If you have a modern apartment that would be expensive to outfit with detail and character, don't even try. Buy an architecturally interesting bookcase, put it against the simple wall, and fill it with beautiful books.

right: Many old buildings, like our loft, include columns and beams that not only support the structure, but also reference the architecture as architecture—reminding you that you're in a building that was constructed with columns and beams. Keep them as they are.

hiptip

If you've got a smallish apartment, try painting all the walls one color. The continuity will create flow and make it feel like a single larger space instead of just a jumble of small rooms.

"Don't focus on what 'goes' with what; instead, figure out what you like, and chances are they will go together. Don't buy all your furniture as a set, or it will look like a set."

high-impact

quick fixes to make any room look better

No two spaces are the same. There's no one universal solution that's going to apply to every oddly shaped room and its finicky owner. But there are common design issues, and knowing a little about how to face and fix them will get you one step closer to a happy, stylish home.

hiptip

Blank canvas: Paint-On Architecture can be applied in a limited area by painting a blank canvas and hanging it—high impact *and* mobile.

think inside the box
paint-on architecture

So often, what you want out of a room is to give it some sense of structure or drama. You want it to look great on its own, but you also want to set it off from the other rooms around it. And in a lot of modern apartments and houses, there's just no architecture to do it: no moldings or structure around the door frames, nothing to make the transition between rooms distinct. A great solution to this is what I call Paint-On Architecture (POA): giving a wall or a room a feeling of structural integrity and interest, not by tearing it down and building it from scratch, but by painting in squares, stripes, bold patches of color that will set off one wall from another. You can do big rectangles of color to give impact to a room. Or just paint one wall its own color to make it distinct from those around it. POA is a great design resource—it's fun and quick and keeps a place looking young. An added plus is that painting only some of a wall, or some walls and not others, means you save money on paint.

paint

pencil

roller

Paint-On Architecture can give style to a stripped-down room with no inherent style. Or you could take a room that's rich in detail and do something that's very cool and modern with it. Make it feel a little bit fresher. POA works great for a loft, too, since what you're missing there is a way to define spaces. The same is true in a lot of new houses or apartment buildings, where, to keep costs down, doorways have not been framed out. There's not a really great way to begin or end painting, because every room just bleeds into the next, without much definition. Paint is a great solution when you need to add that definition.

It's easy to do. If you manage to buy a roller and some paint, and you own a level, tape, and a pencil, you're good to go. The projects can get very complicated (intricate stripe patterns, matching colors between rooms, etc.), but in its simplest form, it's a time-saver, because you don't have to paint the whole room. There are lots of ways to tszuj a place with paint—exaggerate the baseboards, paint in your own door frames, put in little fixes where drama is lacking.

5 Ways to Try
Paint-On Architecture

Try a rectangle of color in the middle of the room. A bright, contrasting color can be dramatic and fun—and it can also distract the eye from the window over there and the unfortunate urban decay lurking beyond.

Have a painting or photograph you really love that's not getting enough attention? Paint a box or strip of color behind it to let it shine.

Paint one full wall a different color than the others in a room. This can make a dull room more interesting, or emphasize part of a strangely shaped room.

Try subtle stripes in a monochromatic range for a more serene, Zen-like effect. Let the colors echo the other colors in the apartment to bring it all together.

Don't have a nice headboard for your bed frame? Paint one on. A dark box behind the bed mimics the cool look of a modern and expensive bed.

straightguyFAQ

Q: **What's the single least-expensive thing I can do to transform my space?**

A: First of all, clean the damn place up, which is pretty close to free. But in terms of actually changing it into something else: Paint. Don't be afraid of color. White walls are not the answer. And don't be afraid of the wrong color—you can always paint it over.

5 Things That Are at Home
in Any Room

A lamp with a dimmer, or at least different settings

A natural-fiber rug

Beautiful art books

A vase filled with something simple and natural

Candles (unscented, please)

Sisal rugs are a great, inexpensive way to add texture to any room, classic or mod. These rough and nubbly rugs are made from natural fibers and are available in pretty much any size you can imagine, with or without a cloth border around the edge. Natural tan is the most common color, but you can also purchase them dyed and even with patterns screened on them. Other natural fibers for underfoot include jute, coir, and sea grass.

hiptip

5 Words You Want to Use
When Describing Your Space
Interesting
Inviting
Comfortable
Smart
Appropriate

. . . and 5 Words You Don't
Scary
Squalid
Rat-hole
Filthy
Biohazard

left: Also at home anywhere is a vessel filled with something natural—and that doesn't just mean cut flowers, which I know a lot of guys aren't into. Instead, try curly willows, sea grass, wheat, or bamboo—either tightly trimmed down stems or long, elegant stalks.

"Understand your space. Ask yourself, What do I live in? Where the hell am I?"

anchor your stuff

Think about a room in which you feel comfortable (in your place, a friend's, wherever). When you walk in, is it clear what the room is used for? Is your eye drawn immediately to where you'd like to sit? A room you think of as comfortable has probably been well anchored. Anchoring a room is something to think about whenever you're arranging furniture. It means laying the foundation of a room. Pick the anchor piece and let that determine how the rest of the room will come together. Usually, the anchor is central to what you do in a particular room. An armoire can look nice in a bedroom, but the purpose of a bedroom is to sleep. So where you place the bed is what counts the most. One of the things we come up against on the show all the time is that most of the houses we see are not really decorated at all. It's not like these guys have made a conscious effort to go for a certain look and failed; they haven't tried anything. So when you enter their rooms, it's chaos. What I do is anchor their spaces around a certain item that makes sense and gives some order to the place.

Q: How can I get inexpensive mood lighting?

A: First off, remember: Incandescent and halogen lights are the only way to go (fluorescent lighting is blue and ugly). Second: Dimmers, dimmers—everywhere dimmers! They change the mood of a room in an instant. Third: The more light sources, the better. New constructions have all these overhead lights, and people think they're done. But the more lamp light you have working with the overheads, the nicer the mood will be. Always have reading lamps next to the bed. For dramatic touches, set spotlights on the floor and uplight architectural detail, interesting furniture, or plants.

straightguyFAQ

5 Ways to Treat a Window

1. Nothing. If privacy is not an issue, and your views are better than the window treatments you can afford, naked is the way to go.

2. Wood blinds. Easy to operate and control light; basic, masculine design; works in both modern and traditional interiors; simple to install; and they come in a range of colors and finishes (but never use plastic).

3. Window shades. Either hand- or string-operated; inexpensive and readily available. Say no to white vinyl, and instead look for natural materials like bamboo, grass, or parchment paper.

4. Roller shades. Perforated shades, made of a solar screen, on a chain roller. They diffuse sunlight while preserving your view, and are a great way to keep your windows architectually clean and modern-looking. Available in rubber or natural fabrics.

5. Prefabricated curtain panels. A great way to soften and frame windows. Unlimited options; easy to operate and install.

5 Quick Cleanup Tasks
Before Company Comes Over

1. Empty the sink of dirty dishes, preferably by washing them. Barring that, just put them in the dishwasher. Or hide them in the oven.

2. Stacks. Got magazines strewn all over your coffee table? Arrange them into a stack. Books on the floor? Another stack. Whatever you can't put away, stack.

3. Use your toilet brush (you do have one of these?) to remove any unsightly discoloration in the bowl. Use a sponge to do the same in your sink and on your vanity. Spray the bathroom with Lysol. All this will take about sixty seconds, and it may be the best minute of time you've ever invested.

4. Air freshener. Even if you think your place smells just fine, you're probably wrong—every man has a tough time noticing the peculiar, even unpleasant, aroma of his own hovel, because he's used to it. But she's not.

5. "Reading" material. Porn of any sort, no matter how soft, should be hard to bump into.

straightguyFAQ

Q: How can I clean my moldy plastic shower-curtain liner?

A: Why would you want to? Throw the damn thing away. Remember: Not everything is worth it, and cleaning a moldy plastic shower-curtain liner is *very* high on the time-and-money-better-spent-doing-something-else list.

5 Ways to a Better Bathroom

1. Clean it. If you watch the show, you know that this needs to be said. There are some nauseating little bathrooms in the world. If you can write your name in the tub, it—and you—has a problem.

2. Add art. Not bawdy posters and other bathroom "art." But a real picture, or a beautiful photograph. Normally you'd put it in the living room, but why not hang it in a place you'll have time to really study and appreciate it?

3. Warm it up. Even pretty bathrooms can be too frigid. All that white and cool tile. Add texture and warmth with a woven wastepaper basket, a bamboo tissue box, or candles.

4. Don't match. Your soap dish doesn't have to match the toothbrush holder. Try a beautiful little silvered dish for the soap, a stylish ceramic vase to hold toothbrushes. Be more interesting.

5. Buy some new towels. It's probably time to do so. While you're at it, bring in a rug. Don't stand around on some fuzzy bathroom mat. Acquire something with character, texture, and color, something not designed to be used in the loo. Try small oriental rugs or woven doormats—think outside the box.

"I hate to talk about 'mistakes' in design choices, but if there's one mistake people make the most, it's **not thinking in terms of personalizing their space.**"

project
the straight guy's house

This is the home of a guy who lives in the typical suburban house complete with two-car garage, 2.1 kids, and all of that. He's a great guy with a great family. But like so many of them out there, he's somewhat lacking in the design department. What wasn't great was the house itself: bland bones, little personality. The occupants had the classic relationship when it came to designing it: He thought her stuff was too dainty and girly, she thought his stuff was too dark and manly. (Well, he did have a thing for taxidermy.) And the kids were frankly embarrassed about the whole place.

My job here was to blend the tastes of the parents and come up with something the kids (and I) could live with. You don't want to take people out of the context of their own aesthetics. Change your look, not your identity.

He didn't like her doilies and quilts and such, and she didn't like his stuff because it was all dead and had faces and eyeballs. But their tastes weren't as far apart as they thought. I married her love of quilts and his love of roadkill, and the love child was patchwork leather (see the club chair at right). Compromise in action. Once the extremes of each partner were toned down, the end result was a home everyone was happy with—even me.

"I married her love of quilts and his love of roadkill, and the love child was patchwork leather. Compromise in action."

the living room

The man of the house didn't really have an idea of furniture, so I introduced him to the look of the Mission style (which, by the way, is totally unrelated to the missionary position)—like the two cabinets in the living room (at right). We also used campaign furniture, which was originally designed to be mobile, to be used by generals and other muckety-mucks in their roving headquarters on their battle campaigns. (This is not *camp* inspired—that's a different project altogether. The two leather campaign chairs are not in the photo—maybe he's off camping with his chairs?)

When putting together a room, look for design echoes, things that translate your own taste in ways you hadn't thought of before. With this design approach, they were able to meet halfway: She had her quilts, and he had his leather. It wasn't as if they had bad taste. They just didn't know how to turn their interests into a cohesive design.

right: The sofa is leather with nailheads, adding texture. I hung the pheasant painting—everyone must have a pheasant painting—above it. The coffee table is something he actually made—birch branches with a glass top.

He called the living room the "Smithsonian Room." I think all the cabinetry reminded him of a museum. They had these lacquered cabinets and a modern black leather sofa that looked like it was taken out of Dirk Diggler's basement. And they had *the* most eight-dollar curtains you can find—that's for *two* windows, four dollars each. Oh my God, they needed help.

Since the house was, architecturally speaking, nothing, the most important thing was to give it some definition. So I Thom-Trimmed the walls. (This is another little trick like Paint-On Architecture.) It's basically Hammer-On Architecture. While it's still easy and cheap like POA, it's better suited to a house like this, where the look you're going for is a little more refined, a little more permanent. I trimmed the rooms out with really inexpensive stock baseboards. I added battens, which are vertical strips of wood, in intervals along the walls. They give the walls some texture and a sense of structure. You can get this wood for nearly nothing at any home-improvement store. But the addition of just this little bit of architecture into this void of design was priceless.

So, for a few dollars' worth of wood that you can nail in yourself, a place can be quickly transformed. After you get some detail on the walls, paint. I did the battens and baseboards in a warm brown and the walls in a light butter color. In the dining room, I kept the butter color for the walls and did the trim in white. You can connect rooms this way just by bringing one or two colors from one room into the next. And the colors worked together, but they also subtly reinforced the theme I was trying to build: that the dining room would reflect her tastes and be light and airy, while the living room would be darker and library-like to appeal to him.

There's nothing wrong with having a beautiful painting of a dead pheasant, but you don't put it in the *baby's* room. The lesson here is that there are things that belong in certain rooms and things that don't.

hiptip

the dining room

In the dining room I chose an interesting Mission-style sideboard and I hung the mirror vertically to give it more height and to play with expectations a little. I used the couple's existing dining room chairs as side chairs, and added two new Mission-style chairs at the heads of the table, to tie in to the living room.

People like things to match, which is too bad; it's so furniture-store-around-the-corner. If you want something to look real, don't buy sets. If it all goes perfectly together, it will look like it came straight from the catalog. If that's what you're going for, okay. But if you want a look that's personal and has depth and suggests that you've traveled outside the mall, skip the sets. Get in touch with your interior interior decorator. Look for things that complement and contrast with one another. Balance hard surfaces with soft edges. Most of all, pick the things you'd like to see waiting for you when you come home each day.

left: I paired down her quilt collection to highlight one specimen artfully displayed on an antique ladder. **opposite:** I installed a sideboard that was in the spirit of Mission design. I even brought in a pheasant (smell a theme?) that the husband had taxidermied, and then added beautiful sconces with candles.

"Don't just buy clothes that people tell you are the things you should have. (Unless it's me telling you.)"

fashion

This may come as a shock, but I don't like the word *fashion*. People throw that term around a lot, and what they mean by it is "of the moment." What's in now, what's out? What's the rage today, and what's so two years ago? But this is *so* not what being a stylish man is all about. My whole philosophy—my personal commitment to help keep you from looking like a complete jackass—is that we all need to find our own personal style. Couture that works for Carson may not be right for you. Don't just buy clothes that people tell you are the things you should have. (Unless it's me telling you.) Your wardrobe should be composed of things that fit and flatter you, things that tell the world something fascinating about your personality, and things that won't embarrass either of us in the morning. You need to own clothes that make sense for the life you lead—but you should also think about how you wish your life *could* be and dress accordingly. Start with classic pieces and tszuj it from there.

My first rule of style is there are no rules. Okay, there are a few rules, actually: Pleated pants are never the answer. Ascots? One in a million of you can pull it off (the rest of you can hold the *-cot* and just say *ass*). And if you ever wear a mustard-colored suit, so help me I will hunt you down and administer some tough love.

People ask me why I think I know everything about fashion. What I politely tell them is that I don't. I know what options are out there and I have an eye for helping people find out what's right for them as individuals. I've always had a thing for clothes. I was the first kid in fourth grade to have Calvin Klein jeans. I quickly graduated to Sasson disco denim and it was all over. I picked out my sister's prom dress in 1979. She was Prom *Queen*, hello! But how my classmates dressed never concerned me too much. I was what you'd call precociously self-involved. I just knew I looked good.

Clothes have always given me the feeling that I can be whoever I feel like being on a particular day. Maybe today I'll get duded up like a Civil War soldier in ratty jeans and a military coat, and tomorrow I'm a latter-day Cary Grant, sans adorable cleft chin, in a classic tailored suit.

One thing that's missing in a lot of people's lives these days is a fashion role model. There aren't many Cary Grants around, and the American workplace has gotten so casual over the last twenty years that we can't depend on our fathers to show us how to pick out a suit and fold a pocket square (what *some* people thoughtlessly call a "hankie"—God, just the sound of that word starts the convulsions—but has much more in common with a fine silk necktie than a snot-rag). Everyone is dressing down, and nobody has any direction. It's like men have fashion amnesia! Come on, it wasn't that many years ago that we knew how to tie a tie, but now guys are running around dressed like hobos. So many people know who they are but just aren't doing anything to shape that message and get it across in what they're wearing. They have no plan. Step one: Have a plan. Step two: If you're among the couture challenged, run for help! If you break your leg, you would go to the doctor. So why are guys afraid to ask for wardrobe advice? And why are they afraid to ask for directions? I sure as hell don't know.

A lot of men whose look doesn't fit them (or the century they happen to be living in) have no idea where to

Q: Why should I care about my clothes being "in"?

A: You shouldn't. You should care about not looking like a jackass. If someone stops you on the street and asks if you're a backup singer for Shakira—and you're on your way into the office—it's time to update your look for something that works for you.

turn. The people closest to them—the wife, the girlfriend, the color-blind parole officer—might not be the most honest or informed sources of advice. Not everybody is as lucky as the men on our show. They have me as their fairy god stylist, on hand to deliver them to sartorial Shangri-la. What you can do at home is select a fashion role model. It can be someone you know, a movie star, anyone who looks cool. Look at what they wear and find out where they get it. Read magazines, ask questions. It's an education, people. Even if you don't like to shop, get to know a good salesman. If he's trustworthy and wants your return business, he'll give it to you straight. Or perhaps he'll give it to you queer—perhaps he'll be a fairy god stylist, too.

Clothes don't have to be terribly expensive to be totally fabulous. Go for things that fit your body and your lifestyle. Investing in key items of quality that won't be the victim of the fickle finger of fashion is money well spent. Repeat . . . After . . . Me: "I am worthy of couture."

Q: Doctor, what's the most common symptom of the style-stunted, and what's the cure?

A: A lot of guys are in a time warp. They hold in their memories a particular moment when they think they were at their peak—usually right out of college, the twenty-five-ish period. They (a) never throw anything out, and (b) never look for anything new. You discovered Bass Weejuns in '87 and you're still wearing them today? It's ridiculous—fashion's answer to Rip Van Winkle. Hold on to what works, but open your mind—and your closet—to new ideas.

5 classics every man should own

1. The perfect suit Still the anchor of a man's wardrobe. See pages 190–196.

2. Denim jacket Rugged, lightly macho, and majorly layer-able. See page 189.

3. Cowboy boots Equestrian kick for your wardrobe, even if you don't ride. See page 183.

4. Cashmere sweater Pornographically pleasurable to the touch, expensive as cosmetic surgery and worth it.

5. Navy blue blazer A multi-tasking, timelessly correct classic. See pages 204–205.

. . . and 5 things you might

survive without, but I wouldn't risk it

A vintage belt

A pea coat

A cool hat

A real tuxedo (not rented)

The perfect leather jacket

shirts
the new ties

Shirts have evolved to a point where they play a much more important role in our wardrobe than they used to. Where once they were the backdrop for a tie, now they are the focal point. White, blue, and pink oxfords are still staples worth owning. But it's the colorful, heavily patterned, woven shirt that's king right now. Most of us have stopped wearing ties to the office and have been missing the extra element of color. Fun, individual shirts can fill that void.

It used to be that the one way a man could express himself in business dress was with a lime-green novelty tie full of elephants drinking martinis or whatever. That was the outlet. It was this narrow little strip screaming *"Look at me! Look at me!"* I don't have anything against ties, but I think it's great now that shirts provide a broader canvas for self-expression. I'm obviously not one for toning it down—have fun with it. Other than skin art, there aren't too many options.

straightguy FAQ

Q: What's the deal with linen?

A: It's a natural fiber in a fairly open weave, great for summer shirts. (And you can almost always see nipples through linen shirts. It's up to you whether this is an asset or a deficit.) Bear in mind that there's absolutely no way to keep linen from getting wrinkled after you've worn it for ten minutes, so don't bother trying: Just use it for those hazy lazy carefree looks of summer.

Striped oxford

The Basic. Don't ask questions—just buy it.

Cowboy shirt

Soft and cuddly. The more worn in, the better.
A multi-tasking, timelessly correct classic.

Blue dress shirt

Like the golden retriever, man's best friend. Dress it up or down.
Makes a great pajama top, too!

Pink

Could pink be the new black? Very likely, but regardless,
everyone looks great in pink.

Something zany

Go ahead—let yourself go! Paisley is fun and sophisticated,
and if it's done in muted tones, you will not look like Paul Lynde,
trust me.

Striped and fun

The most versatile shirt in your wardrobe. Wear it with a suit and tie,
jeans, or paisley capri pants. (Just kidding about the capris.)

Gingham

Fresh. Classic. Cute. Avoid red-and-white gingham,
as you'll inevitably look like the host at your local Bob Evans.

Denim or chambray

See Robert Redford. Hot.

Knit button-down

Neat knits are a cool alternative to tradition woven button-downs.
A little more sexy. Try it; you might like it.

When you're ironing the collar of higher-collared shirts—you're ironing your own shirts, right?—make sure you iron the collar laid-flat completely open, from the back side (the side you can't see when the collar is folded), so that the top gently rolls and isn't sharply creased. Oh, but wait, you say you're not ironing your own shirts? Didn't think so. Ask your cleaners to pay special attention to special shirts. **hiptip**

carson's brief history of shirt wearing in america

In the 1940s and '50s, life was simple: You wore a white shirt with a red or black tie. A few color options crept in, but the real action came with the arrival of the novelty ties that emerged suddenly in the '70s. Then novelty ties wore everyone out. And then ties disappeared altogether. All of a sudden it was like "Oh my God, that white shirt looks so boring all alone—let's do color!" Remember how color was so, like, seven years ago? Then gingham. Everybody in freaking gingham! (If any of you straight guys don't know what gingham is, think picnic tablecloths; think what Mary Ann generally wore on *Gilligan's Island*.) Two years ago, stripe madness hit our shores. Stripes have taken over to the point where I am almost over stripes, which truly scares me because I love stripes.

The good news about cool woven shirts is they easily make the transition between going to the office and going out for the night. Having all these options means you have to think a little more with these shirts than you did in the days of the plain white shirt. But it pays off in terms of style and flexibility. I love a stripy shirt, worn open at the collar with just jeans, a great belt, and a nice Italian loafer. A great easy look that you can put on after work.

Q: **Can I put a striped tie over a plaid shirt?**

A: Mixing and matching is all about scale. The trick, and not the rule, is: Keep both garments in the same color family and let the patterns vary in scale. Try a bolder check on your shirt and a finer pattern in the tie. Or vice versa. When in doubt, err on the side of smaller patterns all around.

straightguyFAQ

2x4
a pair of shirts, a host of options

Like a good prom date, shirts will go anywhere you like and do whatever you ask. Pull them together with a tie for work, or unbutton them for a night out. More styles out there mean more combinations and fewer rules. A word of advice: Even if you mostly wear your shirt open and informal, do buy the correct size for your neck, so in case you decide to wear it with a tie you won't end up looking like your neck has been piped through sausage casing.

Q: Can I wear a wife-beater under that pretty shirt?

A: Please, we call them "domestic-partner-beaters" in my house. One reason for a buffer zone under a dress shirt of fine cloth—150-count cotton or higher—is that you can see through it a bit. Body hair is not an attractive sight, but neither is the scoopneck of your 'beater. So the answer: No, wife-beaters are so rarely the answer. Wear a proper crew-neck undershirt.

straightguyFAQ

1. Stripes can add sartorial sass to your suit and tie. More fun than a barrel of credit cards.

2. Worn open with denim. Dressed down but still dressed up. Don't forget to tszuj the sleeves to show some skin, people.

3. With a blue blazer, the striped shirt becomes the new tie.

4. When paired with a V-neck sweater, the touches of color at the neckline and cuffs will keep you from looking like a math major.

1. Dressed up with a blazer. Ivy League chic. From desk to dinner in one fell swoop.

2. Preppy is as preppy does. Handsome!

3. L.A. cool, with a long-sleeve tee and denim.

4. Worn under the suit, the polo shirt elevates "dressy casual" to just plain cool.

care and feeding
Instructions for your fabulous shirts

Loosen up. Go crazy, America: Ask for your shirt unpressed. Imagine the straight male bringing home his freshly laundered shirts and . . . they don't feel and look like cardboard! Is it too much to dream? We, as a gender, overstarch. The more woven, casual shirts you work into your wardrobe, the more vital it is for you not to treat those shirts like the stiff, formal things you might be used to wearing under a suit. There's nothing I hate to see more than a guy with a nice stripy shirt on under a blazer, stylishly open at the neck, but stiff as a board and horribly creasing and crackling from all the heavy pressing. (Heavy petting, yes! Heavy pressing, no!) If you're wearing a sport shirt, treat it like one.

Here is another heresy to freak out your anal-retentive dry-cleaning fiends: Your oxford shirts can be washed at home. It's actually better for them, as they benefit from more abrasion, getting softer and cuddlier with every wash. But true dress shirts—ones you're going to wear with a suit and tie—should be sent to the cleaners. I'm a fan of light or no starch. Starched shirts actually show more dramatic wrinkling than their relaxed untreated brethren.

I don't recommend wearing an undershirt with sportier shirts. You'll just look like a geek (pocket protector not included). Wearing an undershirt with a dress shirt feels good against the skin and protects the higher-quality cotton shirt from sweaty-pit syndrome. Clean your unprotected sport shirts after every wearing, and your undershirt-protected dress shirts every other time, depending on how your drooling problem is coming along.

someone's
been very knotty

what knot to do

A lot of fashion books and magazine articles claim that different head shapes and sizes are best framed by specific shirt collars. Nonsense. If you have a teeny little pinhead, then maybe you don't want an oversized Gucci collar—you'll look like Ichabod Crane. Or like some horrible Maude–Ichabod Crane hybrid. Then again, if your head is in that much trouble, no Elizabethan collar is going to save you. This is a make-better book—we're not licensed for cranial transplants.

There's no one-size-fits-all rule. Try the shirt on and see how you look in it. If it flatters you, go for it. The only thing you do have to remember is when tying a tie, make sure to balance the size of the knot with the dimensions of the collar. An oversized full Windsor knot would overwhelm a whispy little collar, just as a thin *Reservoir Dogs* tie would look lost in the shade of a big, Italian collar. Balance the scale of the tie with that of the collar and you'll be fine.

hiptip

Feeling blousy and lousy? Some shirts, especially American made, are too wide around the middle. Have your offending oxfords trimmed by a tailor for a nice narrow fit.

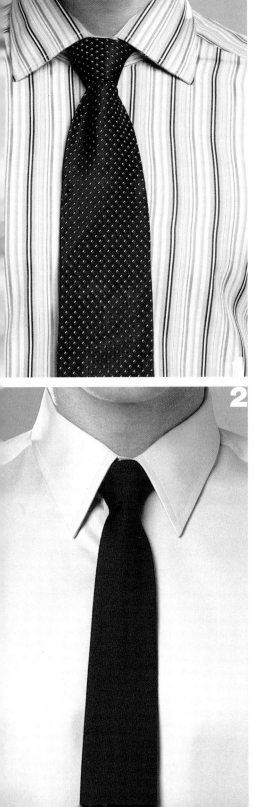

"When tying a tie, make sure to balance the size of the knot with the dimensions of the collar."

1. Big Italian collar: Use a double-Windsor.

2. Point collar: Go lean, with a four-in-hand.

3. Spread collar: Use a half-Windsor.

better living through accessories

Clothes may make the man, but accessories make the man fabulous. Look for the details that let your inner elegance, sly wit, and winning personality shine through. Go for flair, not flash. Flash is garish and screams for attention (would I ever do that?). Flair, on the other hand, is about a stylish tweak, the right little tszuj that doesn't ask for attention—but gets it.

Edit your wardrobe. Just like the food in your fridge goes bad (you knew this, right?), after a while you need to throw out clothes that may have spoiled. If you've built a wardrobe around classics, peppering it with some fun twists, you won't have much cleansing to do. An easy rule of thumb: If you haven't worn it in over a year, throw it out or donate it to charity. Keeping those jeans that don't fit you anymore as inspiration to diet? Cute. But Weight Watchers is more effective.

The Man Bag

Anything too small to hold a laptop computer is going to look too feminine. And anything that looks like it was meant to carry a laptop is going to make you look like a math major. Invest in leather. A good litmus test for a bag is to ask yourself: If I saw this sitting unattended at an airport, would I call security, or want to steal it? If theft is the answer, that's your bag.

Sunglasses

Everyone should own at least one pair of killer shades. Ray-Ban Aviators look great on almost everybody. Steer clear of "sports" sunglasses that make you look like a fly. Avoid dark tints—you'll wind up looking like Ronnie Milsap. Looking like a blind country singer from the early eighties is so rarely the answer.

Belts

Personality starts in the crotch region. But *you* knew that. Get a vintage leather strap and find a belt buckle that says something about your personality. If you don't have a personality, try a Disney character. Thumper, perhaps?

Pocket Squares

Ralph Lauren always says "last thing on, first thing noticed." If you're wearing a blazer without a tie and you have your shirt open at the collar, you need that touch of color, of contrast and flair, that a pocket square provides. There are so many kinds out there—micro-dots and checks and wild paisleys—you've got to have fun with it. Here's your license to tzsuj.

Watches

If you're like most guys, you wear very little jewelry (unless you're a hairdresser, in which case you likely don't need this book). The one bit of bling you're going to invest in will probably be a watch, so why not make it a great one? Even though this is an area in which to shine, I don't recommend gold for most men. Steel and silver will stand the test of time.

Cuff Links

A great way to inject a bit of dash and humor into your wardrobe. They're so personal, like jewelry, and flea markets and antiques stores are filled with interesting, inexpensive variations.

Collect call for Mr. Technology Guy: Cell phones are not accessories. Take it off your belt, now.

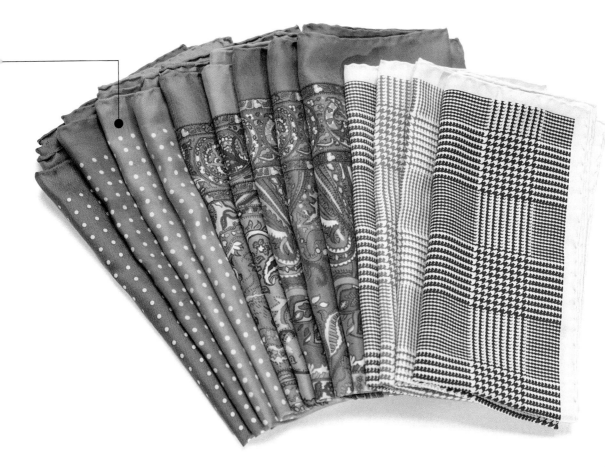

Q: Which of my T-shirts should I keep and which should I dump?

A: I hate to see guys going out and buying T-shirts that say JOE'S DONUT SHOP, PEORIA IL—and they're brand-new off-the-racks from some mall shop. I'm all for having a collection of fun T-shirts, but get the real thing. Fake vintage tees, like palazzo pants, piss me off!

five pairs of shoes

every man should own

Your shoes and your bed are your two most important purchases in terms of sheer comfort level. The secret to purchasing shoes is to keep things simple. Footwear is that rare realm where you want to keep tszujing to a minimum. Shoes are not the place to get funky. You can be somewhat creative with color, but not with construction. Avoid choosing something that's going to land you in the emergency room with that cute podiatrist, Karl.

Quality over quantity will serve you well here, too. You don't need a closetful of shoes: You just need a few well-chosen pairs to get you where you need to go. Look for natural materials and quality construction. A lot of expensive designer shoes are shoddily made. Smell the leather, kick the tires. Buy the best that you can afford. Shoes are like sex: It's going to require a little experimentation before you realize what makes you feel good.

Wear it with:
Gray pinstripes
Khakis and cashmere
Levi's 501s

Wear it with:
A black poplin suit
Black khakis
An Ivy League education

Wear it with:
Corduroys
Linen shirts
A Maserati (just a suggestion, people)

Wear it with:
Techy nylon
A slim navy suit
Everything

Wear it with:
Vintage denim (duh!)
Military cargoes
A tuxedo!

denim and beyond
it's a very denim world

Once the wardrobe workhorse of farmers and coal miners (and folks who wanted to look like farmers and coal miners), denim is now de rigueur for rock stars, wannabe rock stars, lawyers, accountants, doctors, moms, pastors, pimps, and just about anybody else with two legs or so. Everybody's wearing denim! And some of them are even wearing it well. The thing about denim is: options, options, options. Knowing which member of the jean family you like, feel comfortable in, and would look good on you is a first step. But the real key with denim is to try it on. There are a hundred different brands with a thousand different names for their various cuts and a million different looks. Denim makers size their stuff differently, and what you want with denim is a really personal fit. A low-rise in one brand won't necessarily fit like a low-rise in another. Try everything on, every time you buy, and you won't be blue.

the many faces of denim

The way a jean looks has a lot to do with what kind of finish or wash is applied to the denim before the fabric is sewn together. Looking at a wall full of jeans in varying shades of indigo can be intimidating. Keeping track of all the different terms for the multitude of exotic washing/grinding/chemical-smackdown treatments can be overwhelming. It's a bit like choosing an engagement ring: There are a million variations, and you don't want to screw it up. Luckily, all you have to remember is to find a color that fits your look and personality. Beyond that, just do me the favor of steering well clear of that heinous splotchy acid-wash option that will make you look like a lost member of Flock of Seagulls.

5 places denim doesn't go

Andy Warhol once wore jeans to the White House. But you're not Andy Warhol. Then again, you probably aren't going to be invited to the White House, either. So, keep this in mind: If you pull together your outfit well, denim can go almost anywhere. Almost. Exceptions include:

1. Funerals

2. Weddings

3. Meetings with loan officers (unless it's a loan shark)

4. Job interviews (unless it's with the Gap)

5. Black-tie affairs—it *can* be done (see page 200), but please, just be careful, people!

Q: What should I look for in a pair of jeans?

A: Fit is personal, but the look of a classic pair of Levi's is never the wrong answer.

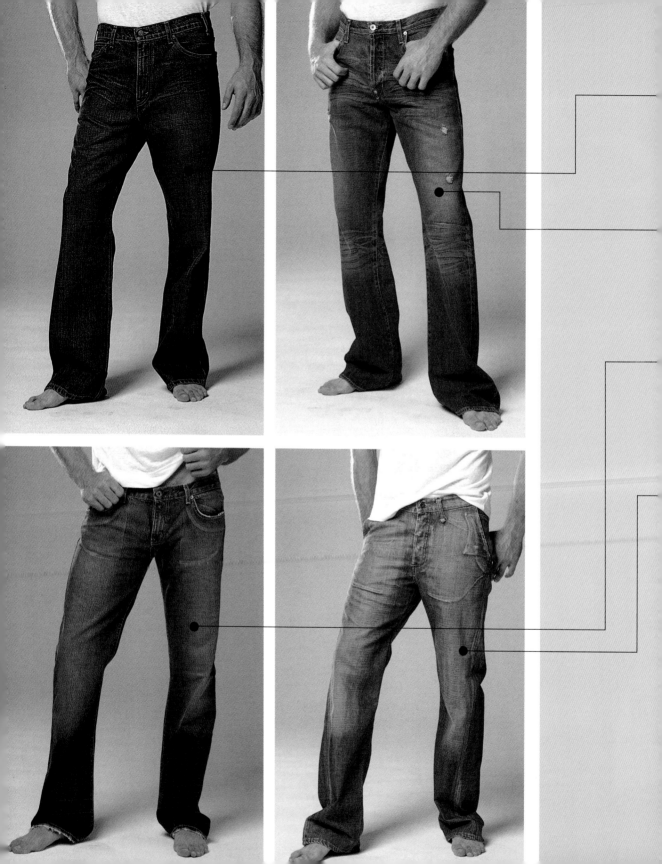

how to buy a pair of jeans

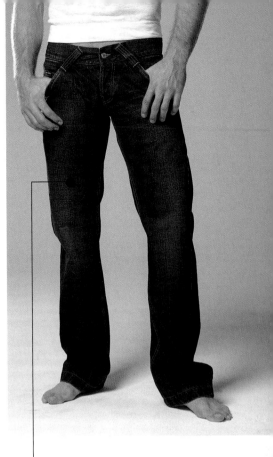

The Classic Five-Pocket

The original, the standby, the old faithful of American male style. Four pockets for your stuff (and one for the pennies you're being paid) speaks to the heritage of denim as utility wear, as rugged manly stuff. These look flattering on almost everyone and are never out of date.

The Boot Cut

Harkening back (as we all like to once in a while) to our Wild, Wild West days. Slightly flared leg to accommodate a boot—or whatever you need to accommodate. Great if you do wear boots. If you're tall, they can create a nice shape. Those on the shorter side risk looking like a long-lost Osmond brother.

The Low-Rise

"Short in the crotch" isn't a phrase you normally want to be associated with. In the case of these low-riding, fashionable pants, though, it's just fine. It's a good, modern, sexy look. But don't overdo it. Rule of thumb: If you can see your pubic hair, they're too low.

The Relaxed Fit

This is a wider fit straight down the leg. A little more casual. A little better if you're a bit on the stocky side, as no jeans should make you look like a stuffed sausage.

The Fashion Denim

These are anything the crazy fashion people want them to be. A hybrid mix of any of the above styles. You could have a low-rise/boot-cut with a special trim, like some leather sewn on for decorative effect. Fashion denim can be exciting and look great, or it can make you look like a backup singer for Shakira. Not for amateurs.

Q: I've heard that I should buy my jeans a size too big and let them shrink—and I've also heard I should buy them a size too small and let them stretch. Which advice is right?

A: Neither. Those are old domestic-partner tales, and the truth is that nearly all denim is preshrunk nowadays. How they fit when you try them on in the store is pretty close to how they're going to fit always. So be happy when you leave and stay happy.

straightguyFAQ

old blue thighs
the value of vintage

Vintage denim is one of the true connoisseur's pleasures. Great jeans age like fine old wine (though they shouldn't ever smell so strongly). It's more than just nostalgia that has us digging through dingy mountains of dungarees looking for that perfect pair. The actual fabric used to be much better made in this country—before we sold off the old looms to the Japanese (that's a long story, but if ever you're offered an extremely expensive pair of Japanese-made jeans, there's a reason behind it). Old denim lasts and lasts. And since the classic shapes and washes are the best, finding a great secondhand pair can be a life-changing moment.

There are two basic ways to find old jeans. First hit the thrift stores, the yard sales, the junk shops, and the flea markets. This is the most time-consuming way to do it, but the tradeoff is the pleasure of rescuing something timeless from the junk heap for a bargain price. A better—but more costly—approach is to find a really good vintage resource: a store that does the searching for you and edits down their finds to a few great pairs. The store's denim specialist (you can tell the denim freak the moment you walk into a store) will have a discerning eye, and he'll save you all that legwork (pun intended).

But remember: Vintage means well-designed and well-made or collectible—*not* just plain-old used. Some vintage styles fetch prices above what some people pay for the suit they get married in: Levi's five-pocket jeans with a capitalized "E" on the label can go for more than a thousand dollars. The range of quality and looks is vast, so go somewhere you trust to narrow down your options. Trying things on—always important in the world of denim—is even more critical in the vintage realm. Sizes vary between manufacturers, between eras, and between individual garments, which have all had different lives. A 34 in one pair might be a 32 in another. Don't sweat the number—you're not working for the I.R.S. here. Just get what looks good on you.

Q: How can I keep the vintage denim I just paid top dollar for looking good?

A: Great vintage denim is actually going to last longer than a poorly constructed new garment because it's made from a better grade of fabric. That said, denim is a cotton product, and it will deteriorate over time. The best way to preserve your investment is to have your precious denim dry-cleaned. It's already soft and pliable—so the washing machine isn't needed to "break it in." You just want to keep it that way.

5 Ways to Incorporate Denim into Your Life

Denim jacket: So many cuts, washes, fits, and quality ranges that it can be quite confusing territory. Go classic here. Novelty denim is almost always the wrong answer. The perfect denim jacket is a vintage Levi's number. Don't worry if it's a little ragged. One person's "tattered" can be another person's "character."

Layer but don't match: Mixing denim is good. Matching the same shades of denim is not. Don't look like a color-coordinated farmer.

Think about length: For casual jeans, a little longer is okay—if the ends fray a bit it will add to the rustic charm. For a neater look, get a size that works for the shoes you'll be wearing. Denim *can* be altered, but do not lose the original hem, which carries a lot of the unique stitching and character of the jeans. To shorten, have your tailor save and reattach the original hem

Dress it up top: When paired with a cashmere sweater or a nice blazer, classic five-pocket denim that's medium to dark is the way to go. Dressing up denim isn't about going with fancy new fashionable styles; it's about keeping it simple and classic.

Dress it down low: White sneakers? Sure, thoroughly appropriate for Beta's kegger bash. Otherwise, try mixing the ultra-casual look of denim with a more sophisticated, adult accent on the feet: Classic wingtips or loafers are perfect. Especially without socks. Dean-licious! (See glossary.)

Q: What's the best bargain in foot fashion?

A: Black flip-flops look chic with almost everything, and you can wear them all summer long. I once sported a $3.50 pair with a couture suit. On CNN, no less.

straightguyFAQ

dr. suits

Men have it so easy! Find a nice, dark suit, make sure you remove the sales tag, tszuj the details, and—whoosh—you're done: instant couture classicism. As much as I like to have fun with what I wear, I like to be appropriate and look correct, too. And a suit never fails on that front. I'll wear crazy things, but that's when I'm barging into straight guys' homes and cleaning out their disgusting dirty underwear drawers. However, when I go to a wedding, I wear a suit. And the dirty little secret of the boring old suit is that they're easy to put on in the morning, fun to wear, and as flattering as any of the most avant-garde couture accoutrements.

This is the staple, the major food group, the big investment. This is where you want to know what you're talking about and get exactly what's right for you. Most people today, because of the casual work environment, won't own more than a couple of suits at a time. Learn about the different phylum of suits and be prepared to shop around. Find a salesman you trust and a tailor you'd take a bullet for.

straightguyFAQ

Q: Daddy, what's a ticket pocket?

A: Your basic jacket has two pretty commodious (that means "roomy," son) pockets on the front, at waist level. A ticket pocket is a smaller, narrower pocket a few inches above the right-hand front pocket, and was designed to hold tickets—back in the days of yore, when travel was glamorous instead of simply yet another opportunity to get strip-searched in public.

the shape of things

It's all about silhouette, silhouette, silhouette. Suits come in a million kinds of fabrics, and it can all be a little overwhelming when you're teetering on couture training wheels. Really, though, there are just a few basic ways suits are shaped. Figure out what they are and where they come from, and you'll be shopping like a pro.

The first flavor to consider is the **Italian form**. Broad shoulders, a little boxy. Often there's no vent in the back where your butt goes. Think Armani. But also think: I do not want to look like a refugee from *The Sopranos*. Proceed with caution.

Next is the **British variety**. It's got double mud flaps in the rear, known as "double vents," the history being that when a man was sitting on a horse, the coat would fall elegantly over the cantle of the saddle. They're also informally called "bugger's delight," but that shouldn't turn you off from this very classic and proper cut.

The **American style** is sometimes called "the sack suit," but I hate that name. It sounds like something ugly and burlap—which this isn't at all. This is the classic Ivy League, J. Press–style suit, with a center-rear vent, and it's one of my faves. Very clean, with narrow lapels and an elongating form.

italian

british

american

double-breasted

There are also **double-breasted suits**—not my favorite, but if you own a number of suits and are tallish and not doing a lot of sitting, it can work for you. But walking around with the double-breasted jacket open, you look like an out-of-work band leader. And don't look for bargains here: The off-the-rack DB is a recipe for disastré.

Something to remember about these generalizations is that they're just that. Since we live in a global, connected, cell-phone kind of world, everyone mixes up the styles like a deejay. Try on examples of all the cuts and see what you like best. Then you'll know what to ask for as you narrow your choice.

Finally, there's the question of how many buttons. The traditional choices are two or three buttons; any more than three is way too Sergeant Pepper.

straightguyFAQ

Q: Which button do I close on my jacket?

A: For a three-button jacket, starting at the top and working down, remember this phrase: sometimes, always, never. For a two-button job, start the phrase at always. If you have more buttons that can be accommodated in these answers, you have too many buttons.

Once in a (Navy) Blue Moon

You own a single, solitary suit. When you bring it out, it's mostly for weddings and funerals. Nothing wrong with that. You work in a casual environment, and you're not in heavy demand as either a best man or a pallbearer. So you need a suit for all occasions, no matter how few and far between they are. Navy blue or charcoal gray are right for you, peanut. Here, we introduce a little idea called K.I.S.S.: Keep It Simple, Sister.

Couture in Training

Maybe you don't even need to get dressed up for work. You just like to. Your gray suit comes out once a week or so for a meeting. The slim-cut navy number with the ticket-pocket and a subtle stripe makes the rounds at night, paired with an open-collared shirt. For good measure, you picked up a khaki poplin all-American suit and wear it as casually as you *used* to slip on your Dockers.

Closet Case

Suited three or four days a week. You didn't buy all your outfits in a weekend. You built your wardrobe the smart way: one piece at a time, seeing what's right for you, what works. Four of your suits are middle-weight all-season models, ranging from a sober chalk-stripe to a bird's-eye, and for a little flair, the smart tweed. The summer-weight cotton in poplin works on sweltering days, and a nubbly, English-cut herringbone keeps you warm in winter. You find yourself admiring the working buttons on your boss's Saville Row suit. You might have a problem.

Sponsoring Your Tailor's Green Card

You wear a suit every day to work and you'd rather undergo a root canal than wear the same outfit two days in a row. You redid your homeowner's policy to account for your expanding sartorial stash: the windowpane blue, glen plaid gray, a nice solid heavyweight tweed, a dashing pinstripe in charcoal. You added a black suit to the repertoire, which can look a bit severe, a bit Amish, but you save it for evenings out and you pull it off. The seersucker is appropriately dandyish and a fun alternative for summer. You haven't told anybody that it was custom-made. You find yourself noticing the stitching on the button*holes* on your boss's Saville Row suit. You need a raise. Or therapy.

evolution of the suited man

Some guys wear a suit every day; others wear a suit just once a year. If you put on a suit once a year, you'll want the most flexible, go-with-anything type; if you put on a suit every day, not only will you want different suits, you'll want different *types* of suits, for different seasons, different occasions, or just different dandy moods. Which type are you? Here are the major categories.

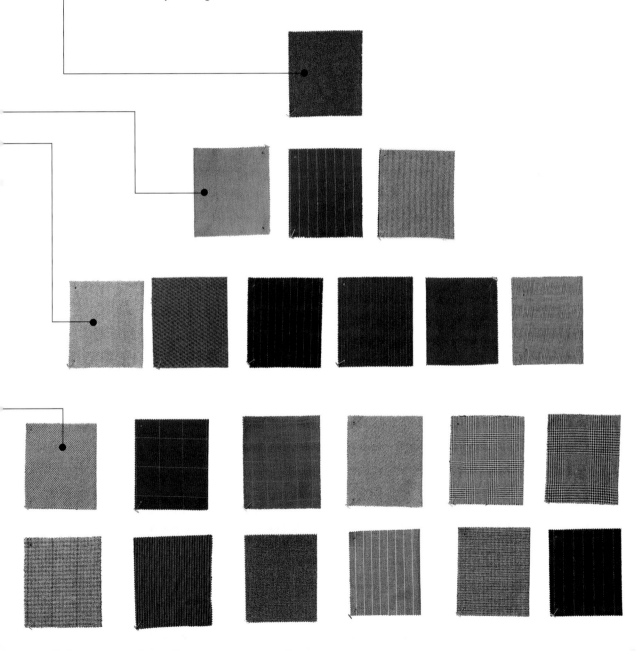

The Kindest Cut

Custom-made suits are the first-class of clothes—no, make that the transatlantic, lay-down-flat-with-slippers-and-wake-up-well-rested-in-Paris sleeper class of clothes. Once you go bespoke, you can't go back. Even if you never have a suit made, you can learn from them. A suit that's fitted closely to the body will always look best. If you've got a big build, a well-tailored suit beats trying to camouflage things with lots of fabric and a double-breasted cut and pleats and tricks. The greatest suit in the world can look terrible if it's badly altered. So no matter your shape, find a tailor who will make your suit really fit you. Off-the-rack suits are sized for the average man, but there is no such creature. God made you unique—just like everyone else.

Q: How wide should my lapels be?

A: Nothing much changes in suit styles. Minor details, but what comes around goes around. Designers these days are taking an old look—that narrow congressman lapel, which comes from the '60s and the whole Kennedy-in-Camelot era—and making it look very chic and modern. There will always be new fabrics and slight tweaks, but if the suit looks timeless to you, it probably is.

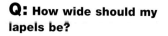

straightguyFAQ

"Clothes may make the man, but accessories make the man fabulous."

black tie
for the
straight guy

I just got a catalog from International Male (*yes,* I'm on their mailing list!). It said something like "Why rent a tuxedo when you can own one for $149?" Remember the Yugo? Do . . . Not . . . Do . . . It. Even if you're going to a fancy dress ball with someone you met on the Internet, you don't order a suit from a catalog.

Black tie is the utmost in elegance, the utmost in chic. Or, rather, it should be. But for reasons that may or may not have to do with the paint-splatter prom-night cummerbunds that corrupted the couture minds of a generation, men seem to commonly mistake "Black Tie Optional" for "Come All Ye Jackasses." There are ways to make the traditional tuxedo fun and show spirit, but they're generally not rentable for $5.99 a night from the local mall's Bob's-Buck-a-Tux.

There's really no excuse for messing up formal wear, because it's so simple. Keep it classic. Remember: K.I.S.S.—Keep It Simple, Sister. And always get a second opinion on your outfit. You're probably not going to the black-tie function alone, so don't step out before letting a responsible party view you in all your formal finery.

dress rehearsal

1. The Shawl Collar A smooth, relaxed look, a certain James Bond-in-the-boudoir appeal.

2. Peaked Lapels The dressiest, most-correct, and hottest option. It's my choice.

3. Notched Lapels New and not improved, the notch is overly like an everyday suit—which contradicts the whole idea of black tie. But it has become the awards-show standard. Go figure.

Advanced Fancy Pants
Tszujing the Tuxedo

The rules for formal wear are not completely, er, black and white. Follow closely and exercise extreme caution; you can go terribly, terribly wrong here. Imagine MC Hammer at an awards show (if he got invited to awards shows).

Wear a dinner jacket with color. Traditional white or ivory dinner jackets are not the only elegant choice. I put a straight guy in a pink jacket and he looked delicious.

Find accessories that relate to an interest or hobby. This is very dangerous territory, but there are very nice, Wasp-ish old-school waistcoats—vests, that is—with tasteful hunting motifs and the like.

Dress your pocket with a beautiful handkerchief. White is standard and will serve you well, but you can try a sassy paisley, check, or dot.

Wear sleek—but not stupid—braces. Suspenders do more than hoist your pants into the crack of your butt; they complete a look. But did you read the part about "not stupid"?

Step out in velvet slippers. Velvet slippers will certainly draw a distinction between the formal and the everyday. Try monograms or any other embroidered message. (Note: This is something of advanced couture maneuver. Not for the fainthearted.)

Go for the haute urban-cowboy look. Wear a denim jacket underneath your tuxedo jacket for a really crazy twist. I just made that one up.

Q: Is it okay to rent a tux?

A: Sure, if you're the type who'd feel comfortable buying a new liver from a vending machine. People! If you have the occasion to wear a tuxedo, it's worth investing in one. They don't have to be pricey and they will never go out of style.

straightguyFAQ

Men seem to commonly mistake "Black Tie Optional" for "Come All Ye Jackasses." There are ways to make the traditional tuxedo fun and show spirit, but they're generally not rentable for $5.99 a night from the local mall's Bob's-Buck-a-Tux.

jackets

Sometimes you just don't want to wear a suit, but you want to achieve a similar level of sharpness as the suit provides. Enter the jacket (in some circles, known as a sport jacket): pretty much a suit, but without the pants. Jackets range from the traditional navy wool blazer and elbow-patched professorial Harris tweed to the rumpled cream linen number, a cashmere glen plaid, or even sleek Italian leather. Americans haven't yet embraced the jacket as European men have—walk the streets of Paris, Rome, or Bremerhaven (well, maybe not Bremerhaven), and check out all those elegantly attired Euro-dudes who are *not* wearing suits. This is something to emulate.

straightguyFAQ

Q: Tell me again why I want to wear a jacket?

A: Sartorial splendor aside, think pockets, pockets, pockets. I have one with eight, and all but one of them (the pen pocket) are big enough to hold my cute little cell phone.

5 blazers to own

Brown corduroy

Navy

Tweed or herringbone

Cream linen

Plaid

blazers are for . . .

Weddings . . . not funerals.

Dinner dates . . . not job interviews.

Movies . . . not the opera.

Graduations . . . not IPOs.

Brunches . . . not brisses.

5 ways to wear a blazer

Relaxed, with a turtleneck and jeans.

Classic, with gray flannels, dress shirt, and tie.

Funky, with a vintage T-shirt.

Collegiate cool, with a cashmere hoody.

Rock 'n' roll glam, with layers of denim.

Q: What's with the gold buttons?

A: First of all, they should be brass, not gold. They shouldn't be shiny, shouldn't be garish, shouldn't look like a rapper's teeth. If they're too shiny for your taste, let them naturally tarnish, or remove them and have them dipped in bleach. Brass buttons are innocuous and traditional, part of the nautical heritage of the jacket, and I think they belong there.

straightguyFAQ

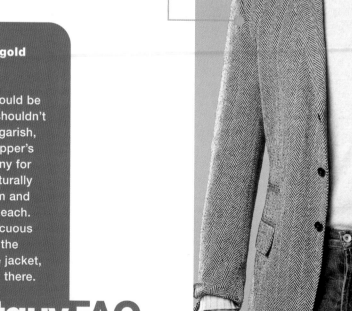

not for amateurs

As we just learned, tszujing our formal wear is a delicate art. In addition, there are some moves only an expert can pull off. You can get there, but it's going to take work, dedication, and long hours of shopping, shopping, shopping. Proceed with caution and pay close attention: The fashion victim you save could be yourself.

Unbuttoned Shirt, Loosened Narrow Tie

A loose and louche look for the right kind of partying man, this can easily stray into schlubby happy-hour-at-Friday's territory if you're not careful. Why start your day looking like you just woke up not knowing who or where you are? **How to work it:** After work, with a drink at a party. Wear your suit to the office, add jeans, open the tie, tszuj the sleeves, boom—you're ready to rock.

Bargain Hunting

A bargain is never a bargain if what you end up with doesn't fit you right, doesn't look good on you, or never sees the light of day. Do not buy something just because it's on sale. Do *not* become a bargain whore. **How to work it:** Carefully. Monitor stuff you like and go after them at sale time. But just like not going into supermarkets on an empty stomach, don't go into mega-sales without a clear idea of what you need.

Sneakers and a Suit

You need attitude to pull this off. And you need the right place to strut it: a party, a funky workplace. Definitely not a wedding. Try this with a traditionally cut suit with a luxury fabric and you'll look like a moron. **How to work it:** This demands a narrow European-cut suit in a modern fabric, or better yet a summer poplin suit. Nothing too fancy or the look is ruined. A twist for winter is a heavier, tweedy but still slim-cut suit with motorcycle or cowboy boots.

The Belt-Over-the-Belt-Loops Look

This is my specialty, and really I have to warn you against trying it at home. You need a sense of rakish angle, of contrasting weights, and a really cool belt buckle. **How to work it:** Honey, don't.

Paisley

Contrary to Elle Woods in *Legally Blonde 2,* some people *do* look good in paisley. I love an old, bold paisley pattern on a man. **How to work it:** Start with a tie or a pocket square. You don't want to jump directly to a three-piece suit all in paisley. Leave that to me or, better yet, Prince.

"Do not buy something just because it's on sale. Do not become a bargain whore."

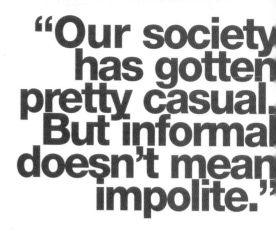

"Our society has gotten pretty casual. But informal doesn't mean impolite."

culture

The other guys on the show have it easy. When we descend upon a straight guy's house like the Gay Calvary, we pick apart every nasty, unkempt part of their home and life. Yes, it's fun. And, yes, it can be scary. Once we're done dumping out their underwear drawers onto the floor (trust me, usually that's a real improvement) and inventorying every item in their refrigerator (usually just a solitary can of beer with a born-on date circa the Quayle vice-presidency), then it's time to put back the pieces and rebuild our straight guy.

That's where my job get complicated. You can fix a guy's hair and tell him what clothes will enhance his physique, but how do you know what's happening inside? I've got to burrow into our straight guy's skull and figure out where his tastes could use some improving.

Culture isn't just about how many opera CDs you own. It's about how many opera CDs you *pretend* to own. Just kidding. Culture means different things to different folks. We are what we're interested in. And while I'm not here to force-feed you high art and tell you to be excited about things you really don't care about, I *am* here to lead you gently to some more options. There's a lot to be interested in out there—up-and-coming bands, tried-and-true art, a book that might be worthy of your attention (and a girl whose attention you might be worthy of). My job is to get you looking and thinking in new directions, which will make you more interesting and, therefore, more desirable.

One of the easiest ways we improve ourselves is just to be open to new things. And the straightest (as well as the queerest) path to that is by simply saying yes. If someone asks you "Do you want to go to—" you can just cut them off and say yes. Rock climbing? Yes. A new gallery opening? Yes. A bookstore reading? Yes. A lot of straight guys can get into ruts of going to the same bars, watching the games with their same friends, ordering in the same buffalo wings. And there's nothing wrong with that comfort. But there's a bigger world out there, and the only way you get to discover it is to say yes.

I like to be social and go places I've never been. I'm pretty open to anything. I've got very few phobias about looking like an idiot. Does it show? Anyway, the point is: I'm open, I'm out there. One night I'll be at a hip-hop club where I'm the oldest person there (really—there are some awfully young clubbers out there), and the next afternoon I'll be at an auction where I'm the only one who arrived by public transportation. I'm lucky enough to live in a city where culture is just out there on the street, like the hot dog carts and the garbage.

New York is great that way, but this isn't about New York: There are a lot of people who live here who don't see it, who are stuck in their routines and worklives, and just don't get out to take advantage of what's around them. I don't blame them—we all have things that distract us, responsibilities that keep us from seeing Swedish films at lunchtime and spending our days thoughtfully wandering the halls of the modern-art museum. But I think it's also a responsibility to keep up on this stuff. Do it because it's fascinating and it will make you more fascinating to others, including, yes, them elusive womenfolk. They're out there at the museums and cafés, the art-film houses and concert halls. Go out and join them.

So many guys I talk to, when they're led into a new situation—tickets to a show they wouldn't have seen on their own, directions to a dance lesson they didn't think they had the heart or coordination to try—what they say to me isn't: "Why did you make me do this?" It's,

"That was cool. I didn't know this stuff existed." Keeping up, staying informed, takes a little work. But there are so many cultural Cliff's Notes out there that none of us really has any excuse for being bored or boring.

The trick is keeping your eyes open—to newspapers and magazines that list and review cultural events, or even just when you're walking down the street—and connecting the dots to what will hold your interest. Your local coffee shop probably has a board with postings of plays, exhibits, and music shows. The newspaper has a calendar of art and cultural events broken down nightly, as well as reviews so you can decide what sounds interesting. The public library probably sponsors all kinds of intriguing lectures, film screenings, and concerts, so sign up for their e-mail list. Finally, guys, put the sports section aside for a moment and go to the arts-and-culture section of the weekend paper for an incredible resource about the goings-on about town—films, theater, restaurants, music, recent books, and even, if you're lucky, a comic strip or two.

The other part of being a well-rounded man is the human interaction part. This is a more complicated dance than anything they teach at Arthur Murray, and a lengthier, harder, and ultimately more rewarding course than anything offered at Harvard. Develop your interests, and you'll be interesting to others. I don't want to make any promises about turning you into an all-star Casanova, but a little culture never hurt a guy's chances. Have fun with the whole self-improvement thing, and you'll be more fun to be around.

However, before I can help you turn yourself into a fun, interesting chap to be around, you have to be a guy who people *might* think is fun and interesting. And that means having good manners. Being polite and considerate, not boorish. Our society has gotten pretty casual. But informal doesn't mean impolite. So let's get back to some basics.

interacting with humans
part 1

Most guys already know how to behave like a gentleman. They just don't *do* it. Their mothers taught them manners, then they went away to college where anything goes, then they got a job and bought a suit and never again held the door open for a woman. Why? Even if you're the smartest man in the universe, with the best clothes and the best pecs and the best job and the best apartment, if you're rude and offensive, no one will care what you've learned, what you do, or how much money you have. They'll just think you're a jackass.

There are an enormous number of situations where exactly how to behave is a little ambiguous. No biggie. I'm not here to tell you the proper title address when corresponding with the governor. I am here to tell you, though, that there is a proper way, and if you find yourself in that position, you should know it. Do a little homework: For example, the *Miss Manners* books by Judith Martin answer these types of questions.

Chances are, you're not sending a letter to the governor (by the way, you'd address your letter to "The Honorable Joe Schmo, Governor of . . ."). But unless you're a scary type of hermit, you are interacting with dozens of people a day.

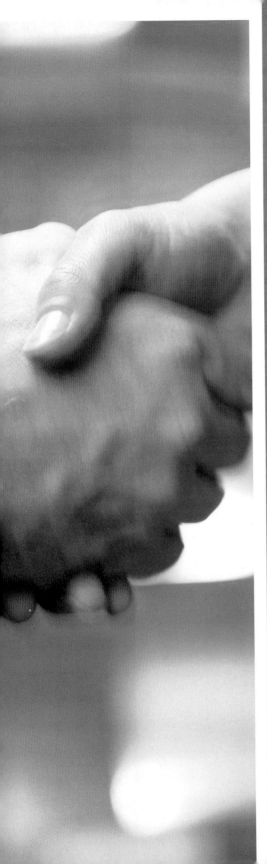

How to Shake Hands

I'm all in favor of the high five, the low five, the knuckle punch, the ass slap, the hair toussle, the cheek pinch (above and below), the elbow grab, the arm touch, the nice noogie, the modified midair arm wrestle, the half embrace, the back clasp, the bear hug with lift . . . Anything that gets people touching, embracing each other, and showing a little love works for me. But there are times when what you need to do is simply shake hands. It's an old and civil tradition, and it would do us all some good to remember how and when to do it.

The grip Strong, not slack. Let 'em know you're there, but don't bring them to their knees in agony. It's not a test of strength, people. Cracking bone is not a sound you want to hear. If it's a man, be firm without being aggressive. If it's a woman, let up on the tension a little to show her some kindness, but don't go limp and make her do all the heavy lifting. Whoever it is, push your hand all the way into theirs, up to the thumb, and grip.

Timing Don't interrupt an intense conversation to shake some-body's hand. Wait until it looks like they're interruptable, and then swoop in from their front—don't sneak up behind someone to shake their hand, or you're more likely to scare the bejesus out of them than to make a good impression.

First meetings The first time you meet someone, shake his or her hand when you're first introduced, and then again when you part.

The host and hostess It's good manners to seek out your hosts as soon as you arrive at the party, and then again when you leave. Shake hands at both junctures.

5 tips for public speaking

There's pretty much nobody who's not afraid of speaking in public—at least a little afraid. You're not alone. Whether it's in front of three people for a dinner-party toast or three hundred people for a sales conference or three thousand people at an awards ceremony, it's a stress-inducing event. Here are five ways to chill out.

Know what you're going to say.

Winging it is really not the answer. It helps to write out your comments, then condense them into quick bullet points, and put them on an index card—just a few words per topic, to jog your memory. Memorize the contents of that index card, and keep it in front of you. You may never need to consult it, but you'll feel better just knowing it's there. But . . .

Do not read word for word.

There are very few people in this world who are great at reading out loud, and unless you're a network anchor or a national politician, you're probably not one of them.

Trust yourself.

You're a smart guy, right? And you know what you're talking about? Yes. So just talk, as if you were talking to one other person. No matter what size your audience, the crowd is still composed of a bunch of "one other persons." Talk to each of them as an individual, not as a mass unit.

Make eye contact.

It sounds like a cliché from some sort of motivational-speaking seminar at the airport motel, but it works: Make eye contact with as many people as possible. Don't *stare* at anybody for extended periods—you're not trying to orchestrate a pickup here. And also don't let your eyes dart around the room continually like a frightened baboon. Try to maintain eye contact for a couple of beats—enough to enunciate a few words.

Breathe.

If "make eye contact" sounds like a cliché, "breathe" may sound like "Duh!" But a natural response to high anxiety is to hold your breath. Don't. You'll rush your words, you'll start to pant, and then you'll start to sweat and feel dizzy. Seriously. I'm not going to get all ashram-yoga on you and start talking about centering yourself with *ohms,* but just remember to take a breath at the end of every sentence. Not only will it keep you physically okay, it'll also help you create a rhythm and slow yourself down. And remember that slower is nearly always better for public speaking.

5 faux pas every straight guy is guilty of

Insulting the help. Waiters, taxi drivers, parking-lot attendants, hotel housekeepers, doormen, the dimwitted clerk at the convenience store . . . if they're not performing their jobs up to your exacting standards, have a little patience. Flipping your lid at a busboy isn't going to make the food come any faster, and it's not going to make you look like a big shot. It's going to make you look insecure and belligerent.

Not giving enough compliments. We gay guys can't understand this at all. If your girlfriend looks especially beautiful, why don't you tell her? If your mom gives you a really great Christmas present? Thank her and commend her for her choice. Or—*gasp*—if your buddy is wearing new shoes that you covet? Tell him so. That's right: You *can* give a guy a compliment, and he *won't* think you're hitting on him. "Cool shoes, dude" is fine. Compliments strengthen relationships by showing you care, that you notice.

Mishandling doorways. Whenever a door opens in front of you—at an elevator, a subway, a set of double-doors in a store, a bus—let people come out before you enter. Even if you're in a rush.

Pretending you know something you just don't. Bluffing is a necessity in poker. But not on a date, and not at a party. If you don't know what in hell someone is talking about, don't pretend you do.

Burping. It's tough not to let out a little beer burp once in a while. And in Japanese culture, it's actually polite to burp after a meal, to acknowledge that the food was good. But not here. Adam Sandler and Jim Carrey might get away with it in on-screen, but when you do it, it's just rude.

the art of the handwritten note

In these days of e-mails and cell phones, of junk mail clogging your mailbox and spam clogging your in-box, everybody likes to receive a handwritten note. As a thank-you for a party invitation or a gift, after a job interview or a good meeting, and 100-percent-without-question-*definitely* after you've spent the weekend at somebody else's fabulous beach house. (In this case, you might even consider sending a gift, too, even if you brought one when you showed up in your flip-flops.) There are tons of stores out there that sell fine writing papers, from unique little gift shops to national chains in malls. Just spend a few bucks on a box of decent paper or cards, and write a note whenever a thank-you is in order. You'll make someone's day.

hiptip

Saying "I'm sorry." It's like a magic potion that dissolves away ill will, simmering resentments, and out-and-out red-in-the-face, dangerous-blood-pressure-level anger. Whatever the disagreement, do you really need to start World War III over it?

Revising the Basic Thank-You

If someone holds the door open for you, say thank you. That person isn't your doorman. (Even if that person is your doorman, say thank you.) If someone compliments you, say thank you. If someone—anyone—does something for you, say thank you. No one will ever say that being too polite is rude, so when in doubt, express your appreciation.

5 hosting tips

The host has special responsibilities—the big ones are making sure everybody has something to eat and drink. Here are some lesser issues that may slip your mind.

Plan your layout, your time, and your help (if you're lucky enough to have some—and also see below) to make sure that every guest has a drink in his or her hand within five minutes of arriving.

Try not to get tied down to one conversation for too long, especially early in the evening. You're supposed to be circulating among your guests, not hitting on that hottie from human resources. (Save that for the end of the party.) If you get cornered, it's perfectly acceptable to be honest: "Excuse me, it was great talking with you, but I really need to make the rounds."

Never provide enough seating for everybody, or you'll have a bunch of people sitting around in little cliques; you want people milling around and mingling, not sinking into a sofa and eyeing your PlayStation. So provide seating for about half your guests—enough to give rest for the weary, while also encouraging mingling.

Dim the lights. If you don't have dimmers for every lamp or overhead, first of all, Thom will yell at you. But more important: Nobody looks his or her best under 100 watts, including you. (And most rooms also suffer from too much light, especially if you've got scratch marks from moving furniture and dents in your moldings from over-aggressive putting practice.) If you don't have dimmers, at least swap out some of the bright bulbs for 40-watters and light some candles.

Hire someone to help. A teenager from down the block, a recent college grad from the office, anyone with the night off who'll be satisfied with free dinner and a few twenties. Although it would be nice to find someone who knows how to mix the perfect Rob Roy, all you really need is someone who can schlep dirty plates, answer the doorbell, carry coats, empty the garbage, run out for more ice, and all the other little tasks that keep you away from your guests—and away from enjoying yourself at your own party. If your budget is tight, remember: It's better to have a two-hour party that everybody enjoys than a four-hour party where the main attraction was you having a meltdown.

5 ways to work a cocktail party

Going to a party, especially a business function or one where you don't know a lot of people, is stressful. Not just for dorks with bad hair, not just for guys who think of themselves as shy, but for everybody. Me, Thom, Carson. (Well, maybe not Carson.) And probably you. Here are some hints to make it less stressful and more fun.

Realize that everybody feels exactly the same way you do, even the hosts. Unless you're attending the one party ever thrown in the history of humanity filled with supremely self-confident extroverts (and if you happen to find yourself at this party—call me!), everybody in the room is feeling at least a small bit of stress.

You should never arrive at a party empty-handed, but what's in your hands shouldn't make demands of your hosts. Flowers that they have to unwrap, trim, find a vase for, put in that vase with water, and find a place to set . . . this is going to take five minutes that they don't have to be screwing around in the kitchen. Ditto anything that needs to be immediately refrigerated, frozen, baked, kept out of the heat, or any other special treatment. And this is definitely not the time to return that piece of luggage you borrowed last summer. On the other hand, you can't go wrong with a nice bottle of wine, especially if it has bubbles.

hiptip

You're not in junior high school anymore, and there are no "in" crowds. That group of guys over there? They're talking about the same game you watched last night. Those two pretty women in the corner? They're just waiting for some guy to come up and talk to them. It might as well be you. It's a party, after all, and people are there to meet other people—be the person they meet. Just walk up, smile, extend your hand, and introduce yourself. You don't need to have a pickup line or a joke or the whole conversation planned out; all you need is your openness. "How do you know our hosts?" is almost always an appropriate question.

As soon as possible after arriving, **say hello to the hosts.** Don't interrupt them if they seem to be engrossed in an important conversation, and certainly don't interrupt them while they're doing something like attending to the flowers someone just bought (but see Hip Tip, left, about this). But if they're just amiably chatting with another guest, say hello. If they're good hosts, they'll probably introduce you to somebody. They may even have a "special" somebody who they want to introduce you to—in fact, that may be the reason you were invited. But you'll never know unless you say hello.

I like a good stiff one as much as the next guy, but **nobody likes a drunk.** Here are two great techniques for keeping your wits about you while still having a good time: First is to make every other drink you have a nonalcoholic one, especially water. Second is to eat, for God's sake. Even if it's just chips and dip, there's sure to be something. Have it.

If you know a few people but hardly the whole crowd, please, please **don't spend all your time talking to your pals.** That's not what parties are for, and you can do that at home. You don't want those two pretty women to refer to you as "those frat boys who spent the whole party talking to one another." So say to your pals, "I think we should probably talk to some other people," and then just turn to whoever's next to you and say hi. That's what parties are for.

"Make every other drink you have a nonalcoholic one, especially water."

Q: If I bring a bottle of wine to a dinner party, and I notice the hosts don't serve it, should I be offended?
MOËT et CHANDON à Epernay
Fondée en 1743
Champagne
Appellation d'Origine Contrôlée
Cuvée Dom Pérignon
Vintage 1990
ALC. 12.5% BY VOL.
PRODUCT OF FRANCE
750 ML

A: No, unless you called beforehand to ask what they'd be serving, and then got Robert Parker Jr. on the phone to find out the perfect wine companion to the meal, and then when you arrived for dinner you announced "The spicy-chocolate overtones in this '89 Château de Beaucastel Châteauneuf-du-Pape will be sublime with your second course of braised short ribs, and I opened the bottle in the cab over to give it sufficient time to breathe, and I even have "these twelve perfect wineglasses here in my pocket . . ." You're the guest, not the caterer.

"Not every cultural wardrobe is right for every guy. But sometimes you should take a chance and try on something you wouldn't ordinarily wear."

body language

Ever catch an accidental glimpse of yourself in a mirror and realize you seem harried and hunched with a scowling look on your face even though you're in a dandy mood? Sometimes we forget that we're visible to other people. That we give off messages with our body—how we're feeling, if we're approachable, if we're horny or angry or haughty or afraid. Most of us don't try to manage these messages, which is a strange oversight given the importance of body language. There's no second chance to make a first impression. You might be crossing your arms because it's comfortable (or because you think it does a good job of covering your beer belly), but the message it sends to the woman at the end of the bar might be that you're standoffish and cold.

Body Language Do's and Don'ts

Do: When you're in a bar or at a party, pay conscious attention to the way you hold yourself.

Don't: Get so distracted thinking about the message your body's giving off that you forget to have actual, verbal conversations with women.

Do: Keep your posture erect, at the very least. It's only the rare guy who can pull off a really cool-looking slouch at a party.

Don't: Keep your posture so erect that you look like an uptight jackass. When good golfers stand at the tee, ready to drive, they often take a little bounce to make their bodies understand that they're fluid things, not mannequins. Try to remember this.

Do: Make eye contact.

Don't: Make eye-to-amazing-breasts contact.

Do: Smile.

Don't: Grimace.

Do: Look at her when she's talking to you—in fact, look at anybody who's talking to you.

Don't: Glance over her shoulder, to your left, to your right, spin around and take a look behind. Give full attention to her. If you don't focus on her, she'll think you're looking for someone better to talk to, even if you're not. If you *are* looking for someone better, you give guys a bad name, and I wouldn't blame her for walking away from you.

learnin' what your mama couldn't know

Cell-Phone Etiquette: 5 No-Nos

First of all, see Carson's tip on page 180—a cell phone is not an accessory. Back in '95, if you had a cell phone, maybe it was cool. *Maybe.* But today, half the adults in the United States have a cell phone. So you're not unique; you're one in a *hundred million.* And if you're making or taking calls in any of the following, you're being rude:

1. On public transportation.

2. In an elevator. Any elevator, even if you're alone. You never know who's about to get on.

3. At a table in a restaurant.

4. On a date.

5. On a job interview.

There really are very few exceptions. If your phone rings, and you just can't let it go through to voice-mail, here's the thing to say: "Hi, I'm with someone, can I call you back?" Simple. If you can't wait the five seconds or five minutes, you probably need a vacation much more than you need to take that call.

> **"Half the adults in the United States have a cell phone. So you're not unique; you're one in a hundred million."**

e-mail etiquette

Do: Respond promptly to e-mails.

Do: Check your spelling and syntax. Even though we all know it's a casual, easy, and disposable form of communication, the message you don't want to communicate is "I'm an idiot."

Do: Remember that e-mails can spread around like wildfire—to your intended recipients as well as to unintended ones like your mom, your boss, and every law-enforcement agency in the world. So don't send *any* e-mails that will ruin your life if that fire spreads out of your control—and you can't control any of these fires, my friend.

Don't: Immediately forward everyone on your list, including your mother-in-law, the picture of elephants doing amazing things to each other. If people want to know where baby elephants come from, they will ask you directly.

straightguyFAQ

Q: Once and for all: Should I hold open the door for women, or not?

A: Yes, hold it open. If they don't like it, and feel strongly about it, they'll let you know, and then you'll know. The exception is the door to the backseat of a taxicab: You should get in first; women don't like sliding across seats, especially when wearing skirts.

the well-rounded straight guy

Leave a book on your nightstand. Just having it there—looking at you and demanding attention like a pet—will do wonders for your reading regimen. A couple of pages before you fall asleep will not only keep you finishing books, it will clear your mind of the day's distractions.

LISTen to the experts

The world is full of lists. Everybody has their top ten favorite movies, the five books they would want if stuck on a desert island, their opinions about the best CDs of all time. Part of being well-rounded is to not simply sit around with your friends and shout, "Dude! How can you even say that Guns N' Roses is the best band ever?" It's also important to expose yourself to some of the classics, to get a sense of the canon, if you will. There are some amazing resources out there to help guide you toward being a better read and more sophisticated you. So take a little tour of some of the most respected Best-Of's from the past century.

book learnin'

When I talk about "cultural Cliff's Notes," I'm not suggesting actually stocking your shelves with the familiar black-and-yellow C-student's guides. This is real life: Shoot for a B+ at least. Extra credit goes to the man who knows a little about a lot. So many of us get to a point where we're done with school and we breathe a sigh of relief and think: Wheeew, that's over. But as long as we live, we're going to continue to learn stuff. There's just no way around it. So drop the notion of homework and think of learning as the exciting opportunity it really is. Tailor learning to what interests you (if you like baseball, read up on the history of the game) and to the bits you may have slept through in

school (history, anyone?). There's nothing wrong with reading spy thrillers or volumes of baseball stats or Dr. Phil's latest advice for getting in touch with your inner bald guy or any of that. But for both the good of your brain and, frankly, the cultural breadth of your bookshelves, you're going to want to branch out in a couple of different reading directions.

That means novels, biographies (and not just the Van Halen story), a little history, maybe even a little science. All the stuff you thought you'd never have to pay attention to after graduation. Some of this stuff is actually interesting. Choose a subject that appeals to you, and don't worry if you think that a full 722-pager is going to be way too much. If it turns out to be, just put it down. But first put down that issue of *Gear* and give the book a try.

The Modern Library publishes an amazing collection of the best American novels. These are the kinds of books that you'd be given if you were to waltz into any bookstore in the country and find a true bibliophile, sit him down, and say, "Look, I need you to give it to me straight: What books are gonna give me the smarts I need and not completely bore me in the process?"

For more contemporary offerings, browse the *New York Times* bestseller list (online at the *Times*'s website, www.nytimes.com) or your local paper's or bookseller's lists. And definitely check out the winners and nominees of major awards: the National Book Critics Circle (at www.bookcritics.org), the Booker Prize (www.bookerprize.co.uk), the Pulitzers (www.pulitzer.org), or the National Book Awards (www.nationalbook. org). These lists represent a combination of the most popular and most critically acclaimed books published—there's something for everybody.

sound off

Nothing wrong with keeping the AC/DC box set in heavy rotation. But just like literature, expanding your knowledge of the culture through avenues yet undiscovered can be a cool and wondrous thing. Next time you're waltzing through a music store, go for broke and grab something you have never considered buying. Pick up a *Rolling Stone* and see what readers chose as the top 100 rock albums of all time. Look on the Internet for the best classical, jazz, or world music.

seeing is believing

Movies get a bad rap for being nothing more than easy entertainment. And it's true that most accredited universities don't give credit for knowing all the lines to *Caddyshack*. But the trick to getting more out of filmgoing is breaking your viewing patterns. *Terminator 17*, for all its charms, is not going to change your mind about anything. But a movie like *Rebel Without a Cause* might.

The American Film Institute published a list of the top 100 films of all time, selected by 1,500 industry experts. These selections not only illustrate the history of film, but offer an incredible look at the hot issues—political, social, and personal—that we've been obsessing over since the invention of celluloid. From the top five (*Citizen Kane, Casablanca, The Godfather, Gone With the Wind,* and *Lawrence of Arabia*) through another two years' worth of Friday-night entertainment, the AFI's list is well worth looking through: www.AFI.com.

Another great way to increase your cultural understanding and have fun while you're doing it is to (and I know it's a cliché to say it) *expand your horizons*. Watch foreign films. And none of that "I hate the subtitles because my TV is too small" malarkey. Foreign films are probably the single best way to understand different cultures, get excited about travel, and push yourself in new directions—all, of course, from the comfort of your couch.

Also try documentaries. The right ones can offer a more exciting, eye-opening experience than a summer blockbuster. Guys, there's a reason you watch reality television shows, and it's not just to learn how to shave. Watching true stories with real people is fascinating, and it will make you more sensitive, more aware, and frankly, more appealing.

Most video stores actually do have great selections of foreign and documentary films. And a good place to start your education is to check out the winners from international film festivals such as Cannes (www.festival-cannes.fr), or the Oscar winners and nominees (www.oscars.org). And it's worth it to pick up the arts section of the newspaper—especially on the weekends, when most papers offer expanded coverage. Read the reviews and go to one of the smaller theaters that specialize in these films.

"None of that 'I hate the subtitles because my TV is too small' malarchy. Foreign films are probably the single best way to understand different cultures."

your cultural wardrobe

Carson won't tell you that every outfit works for every guy, and I'm here to tell you that not every cultural wardrobe is right for every guy. But sometimes you should take a chance and try on something you wouldn't ordinarily wear. But know your limitations: Don't sit through three hours of *The Iceman Cometh* if you can't make it through an NBA quarter without checking your voice-mail messages. There are one-act plays, forty-five-minute recitals at music colleges, and one-artist gallery shows. These are all things you can do after work and before dinner. And whether you're in New York or North Dakota, that talented lead may be an Academy Award winner in five years.

Opera Try a "beginner" opera—*Carmen* or *La Bohème,* for example, or something else with a lot of recognizable tunes. But certainly not anything grave like a four-and-half-hour Wagner wrist-slitter. If for no other reason, there will be large-breasted women on stage, heaving. And, sometimes, Vikings.

Go back to school. Take a date to a wine-tasting class, a cooking class, a dance class. Shared bond, shared knowledge, shared everything. You might even enjoy the homework. A+ for effort.

going to the theater doesn't mean you're gay
5 superior alternatives to the dinner-and-a-movie dulls

Theater There's something about seeing human beings live, in person, just a few feet from you, that just can't be matched by movies or television. Plus, if you do your homework, there's always the possibility of finding a play with nudity.

Get outdoors and/or physical. Do something active—hiking, sailing, tennis, or just renting a rowboat in the local park (or, if your forearms are too spindly for even rowing, just have a picnic). Or full contact putt-putt.

"Haven't you always wanted to . . . ?" Take a helicopter tour of the city or a hot-air-balloon tour of the country? Have a dinner composed entirely of desserts? Wake up before dawn to watch the perfect sunrise while drinking champagne? Tell her you do, and ask her to come with you. This is something you'll tell your grandchildren.

interacting with humans

part 2: the opposite sex

"Love," the great jazz singer Billie Holiday sang, "is like a faucet; it turns off and on." She might have added that it also sometimes gets rusted up, clogged, and corroded when badly neglected. Most of us don't have a problem knowing how to fall head over heels, note writing, tattoo-her-name-on-your-chest-before-you-know-how-to-spell-her-last-name stupid-actingly in love. The problem is upkeep. Love is not a Volvo that runs for a hundred thousand miles between tune-ups. Love is a finnicky Jaguar, or a ouchy, feisty Italian number (somewhere between a Fiat and a Ferrari) that gets hot under the hood, demands attention, needs tune-ups and new hard-to-find parts.

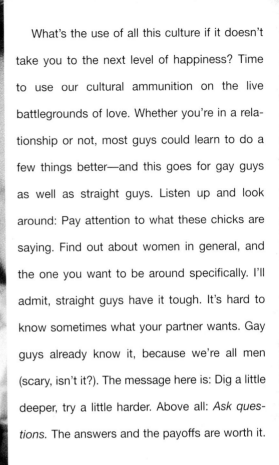

What's the use of all this culture if it doesn't take you to the next level of happiness? Time to use our cultural ammunition on the live battlegrounds of love. Whether you're in a relationship or not, most guys could learn to do a few things better—and this goes for gay guys as well as straight guys. Listen up and look around: Pay attention to what these chicks are saying. Find out about women in general, and the one you want to be around specifically. I'll admit, straight guys have it tough. It's hard to know sometimes what your partner wants. Gay guys already know it, because we're all men (scary, isn't it?). The message here is: Dig a little deeper, try a little harder. Above all: *Ask questions.* The answers and the payoffs are worth it.

5 places to look for love

You've been burned one too many times by Internet dating. The only thing you pick up in bars is the tab. You're not quite ready to hang around widow's support groups or give the green light to the arranged marriage with your grandmother's mah-jongg partner's niece. Where can you go to get lucky without that icky meat-market feel? While there's no surefire solution, the best advice is to put yourself in the way of women. (But note that this doesn't mean running in traffic and throwing your body onto the hoods of their cars—though if she's really hot and she looks like she might hit the brakes in time, hey . . .) Here are a few places to make yourself visible.

1. Volunteer groups and other organizations Join one, whether it's the local coat-drive or elder-companion program (and, possibly, most any organization that helps other people will give you huge rewards that have nothing whatsoever to do with romance). Or your local chapter of Road Runners or even the U.S. Chess Club. Whatever your interest, there's probably an organization out there for like-minded people. (Unless your interest is dressing up like Mean Joe Greene and re-enacting that Coke commercial from 1984, in which case you're probably on your own.) And wouldn't it be nice—in fact, wouldn't it be *ideal*—to find a woman who shares your passion?

2. Specialty shops Drop in at a book store, especially during a reading, and maybe you'll learn something, too. You may visit Sports Authority and the Gap every once in a while when you need something, but women shop for *sport.* Find the street with all those upscale specialty shops—for food, wine, linens, furniture antiques—and just wander in and out of them Just don't linger too long in the lingerie store or you might end up having a little chat down at the station.

3. The gym It's an obvious call—you'll be surrounded by scantily clad chicks sweating. A couple tips to remember, though: Don't be aggressive—people expect and deserve their privacy in a gym, so this is no place to put on the heavy moves. If there's a particularly cute girl taking a Pilates class that's always scared you off, give it a shot. The worst that can happen is she'll see you making the effort—and getting buffer as you try.

4. Coffee shops The new singles bars. Why do you think there are so many people here hanging around if not to meet someone? There's only so much caffeine a body can handle in a day. Take your weekend paper, a good book, your laptop, a magazine, or whatever will give you some light distraction. Sit by yourself at a table that seats four. Sooner or later, women will sit with you. As long as that magazine isn't *Playboy*.

5. Museums Don't laugh. Trust me, chicks—especially hot foreign ones—*flock* to museums. Just make sure that thing you're thoughtfully staring at is a Post-Modern installation and not actually the bathroom door.

Ask her out. Just do it. What's the worst that can happen? "No." You're not going to lose money, she's not going to yell at you, and you're not going to get beat up by her gigantic boyfriend (unless the gigantic boyfriend is standing right next to her when you ask, in which case you're not too bright, are you?). Remember: It's not the games we lose that we end up regretting; It's the games we don't even play.

hip tip

5 great straight-guy cultural weapons

I know what boys like, which is lucky for me. But you, my friend, are trying to write a novel in a language you don't understand—the language of the opposite sex. You are a deaf guy composing symphonies (oh, wait, that's been done). My point is that being a straight guy is rough because you have to be an interpreter of women. So get out there and equip yourself with the information to be the best straight man you can be.

1. Read *Cosmo* or something like it. In just a half hour of browsing through a women's magazine, you'll learn more about women—what they want, what they need—than a decade's worth of lamenting chick behavior with your buddies at the bar. The trick is actually reading the articles and not just looking at the pictures. You'll find information on fashion, women's anxieties, more fashion, trendy new orgasms, more anxieties, and the latest trends in undergarments. Sure, *Maxim* will expose you to hot babes, scantily clad. But *Self* will expose you to how to actually talk to those hot babes.

2. Watch "chick flicks" for clues to what makes them tick. Surely there must be inside information in *Sleepless in Seattle* (as lame as it is). Educate yourself on the grand gesture by watching *Casablanca*. Learn about having fun on the back of a Vespa with a woman of superior social class in *Roman Holiday*. Watch anything with Cary Grant for clues on how to be a sly womanizing cerebral stud—and have them love you for it.

3. Read a piece of chick lit. *Bridget Jones's Diary, The Girls' Guide to Hunting and Fishing,* or nearly anything on the fiction bestseller list that's written by a woman. Read the flap copy, and read the first five pages. You might want to try doing this in a city where you don't know anybody.

Sometimes gifts are gestures, and gestures don't have to be grand. Do something for her that you won't be around to take credit for or share in. For example, if she's traveling alone, call the hotel and have them send up a bottle of champagne. Or slip a note and a little gift into her luggage, something she'll find when she arrives. It will make her think of you—and think better of you.

hip tip

4. Keep up to date. Planning engaging dates, making good conversation, and being an all-round interesting person to sit next to on a plane—none of these comes to you by accident. Being interesting means being involved in the culture. Keep up to date with the arts coverage of magazines and newspapers. Reviews and profiles will give you background info and talking points, listings will give you ideas of upcoming shows, openings, debuts, and other hip happenings.

5. Take the next step. Attend some of these upcoming shows, openings, debuts, and other hip happenings. You'll be all the more interesting.

catch her if you can
a sane man's guide to creative stalking

Stalking gets a bad rap. Sure, it's *technically* against the law. But so is insider trading, and that never hurt any . . . oh, wait, I guess it did. The point is, doing a little recon can be a good thing. The more information you have, the better equipped you are to deal with any contingency. Do you want to wait until your wedding night to find out that your new father-in-law was just released after a ten-year term for castrating her high school boyfriend? No, you don't.

Intelligence Report

When you're buying a stock or betting on a sports team—or whatever kooky things you straights are into—you read up on them, you do your homework, right? Same should go for a date or a mate. Find out everything you can from her, from her friends, from how she dresses to what she talks about. You can ask her friends questions about her. You probably shouldn't call her parents for tips to bed her, or call your buddy at the FBI for a full background check. Be attentive, not a freak.

Q&A

What's the easiest way to find out what she's like—what she hates and what she loves, what she reads and what she listens to, where she's been and where she's going? Ask her. Just say, "What do you like to read?" But don't make this an inquisition—for every question you ask you should also work your answer into the conversation.

5 birthday presents to make her swoon

Like the arts, women take some studying before you can fully, er, grasp them. Know your subject. And remember that presents aren't just for birthdays and holidays, when she's also collecting loot from lots of other people (her best friend buying those new boots she wants, her father maybe giving a car). The most meaningful—and memorable—gifts can be those "just because" ones that she's not expecting.

1. A trip. Take her away somewhere, anywhere. Paris. Passaic. Pasadena. She's impressed and you get her all to yourself. You cannot go wrong with this.

2. Pampering—massage, manicure, a day at a spa. Ask any woman you know what the best place is for this—they all know it—and buy her some TLC.

3. Something that she once mentioned she liked. This is perfect when it's something she forgot that she ever told you. You romantic, you remembered it. (But this should not be an ex-boyfriend, and *definitely* not a three-way.)

4. Cancel your plans and give her your attention. Skip the poker group, TiVo *Queer Eye,* and just spend time together. Works every time.

5. Diamonds, diamonds, diamonds. That works too.

Do her job. Think about what you'd really like: Someone to relieve you of some bit of your daily drudgery. It's thoughtful. It's selfless. It's free. Do it every once in a while, too, not just on birthdays or when a gift is expected. Take the kids to school. Do the laundry. Make dinner. Whatever it is that she thinks is her job, just do it.

hiptip

tszujing the date
5 paths to turn a date into a mate

So, you've cleaned up your act and now you've found someone you really like. Dating isn't just time together, it's a chance to show your interest, your creativity, and yes, your newly broadened horizons. So don't squander it on a cliché date.

1. Make it personal. Here again the key is information. Find out what she likes, what she hasn't done in a while or has always wanted to try, and incorporate this into your date. This doesn't mean everything's got to be super-choreographed or complex. Just follow her lead. If she likes dogs, a day at the dog show isn't going to kill you. Let her see that you've listened and reap the rewards.

2. Make it outside. From a picnic to an open-air concert, to a summer's drive with the top down (the convertible, not hers), there's something nice about just getting out in the elements. Sun and air and even wind and rain can be sensual to experience together. Just be sure to give her advance notice about which elements might be encountered: Nobody likes to wear high heels on a bog walk.

3. Make it cultural. Plays, museums, lectures—these work as dates on many levels: They're interesting, they're classy, they give you something to talk about, and they save you from the total cliché of dinner and a movie.

4. Make it active. Staring into each other's eyes by candlelight is great—if you know each other pretty well. But early dates especially are about finding out about each other, something that can be hard in the vacuum of the typical romantic date. So do something fun, play a sport, see each other sweat, or face a challenge. You'll have much more to talk about when it's time to make goo-goo eyes over dinner.

5. Make it your own. One reason guys sometimes feel like a fraud on a date is that they're living someone else's idea of a good time. I'm all for trying out new things, but if you're planning a date, choose something that really reflects who you are and not what you think you're supposed to be. Show your true colors—you'll relax and if she doesn't like the real you, better to know now than six dates later.

If you want to get out there and learn a new dance—and have a great time while you're at it—many nightspots offer hour-long tutorials before the actual night of dancing begins. Try something structured like Latin or swing, which both work with simple counts; you can learn a lot in that one hour. A dance lesson is a great thing to do with your date— a shared learning experience, a night's activity, and a lot of intimate touching. But it's also a great way to *find* a date: The women at these classes are always looking for fresh partners.

hiptip

gotta dance!

It's not just about dance. It's folk-music concerts or sky-diving or whatever it is she really likes to do and you really can't stand the thought of. Men who don't like to dance, I feel your pain. You're ungainly and uncoordinated and unsightly and, yes, the truth is you do look like a fool out there on the dance floor. And you know what? That's okay. Dr. Jai is here to tell you that bad dancing is not a life-threatening condition. (*Not* dancing, though, could be.) Bad dancing is usually reversible, and even when therapy fails, the worst that happens is the patient gets his freak on a little too freakily and charms the ladies with his effort and enthusiasm.

Dancing, to paraphrase Woody Allen, is 98 percent just showing up. Does it matter that you don't know how to dance? Does it matter that you don't really get into it and there are things you'd rather be doing than wooing cheek to cheek (you pick which cheeks)? It does not. What matters is that you show your woman that you're flexible (even if not literally) enough to try new things, to do something she wants to do. It doesn't have to be pretty.

So the next time she wants to try out a new club or do a new dance, say yes, close your eyes, and shake your ass like a man.

glossary

aesthetics: Style awareness, taste.

anchor: Term used for the piece of furniture or architectural detail that becomes the focus of a room. A sofa against the wall can anchor a room. A bag of half-eaten potato chips on an ugly futon cannot.

ascot: Pretentious anachronistic assoholic neckwear. Carson says "Don't."

astringent: Product that closes pores, preventing dirt and grease from seeping in.

b&t: Bridge and Tunnel. Meaning people with bad taste who come via bridge and tunnel from places like Brooklyn and New Jersey to Manhattan. Does not refer to *all* outer-borough residents, just an unfortunate style of dress and manners.

bar soap: Dries out skin. Okay for use on armpits, not for faces. See, instead, CLEANSER.

black tie: Wear a tuxedo. *Not* a nice blue suit: a T-U-X-E-D-O. Someone may want to take a picture of you with a lot of other guys wearing tuxedos, but if you're wearing the blue suit, they'll instead ask you to get Aunt Sylvie another Midori cocktail.

black tie optional: Invitation instruction that translates to "For God's sake, try to look presentable." No jeans, no FUBU sweats, no flip-flops. If you don't have a tuxedo, wear a dark suit and behave.

blazer: Sports jacket. Usually refers to a classic navy-blue standby.

body language: What our bodies say when we're not paying attention. Closed stance or sensuously welcoming? Berlitz for body language may help you communicate with the opposite sex.

boot cut: Style of jeans, with flaired legs originally designed to allow room for cowboy boots.

bouquet: The smell of wine. Swirl the glass, sniff the stuff, and smile. Telling people what you smell is the first step toward wine snobbery and should be undertaken with extreme caution.

boxers: Great for ventilation, not great for slimming figure. Underwear best worn by the youthful and the elderly. Try BOXER BRIEFS instead.

boxer briefs: Supersized tighty-whities. Cottony, comfortable, and classic.

cashmere: Butter-soft fiber from the belly of a goat. Makes the best sweaters.

chambray: Soft fabric resembling denim.

chardonnay: Grape from which white wine is made. Much of it comes from California, Australia, and the French region of Burgundy. *So* 1986. And also immensely difficult to pair correctly with food, and overpowering to many palates.

chef's knife: Kitchen MVP of all time. If you plan to make anything more complex than a bowl of cereal, an 8-inch knife is a culinary necessity. Spend the money on a quality blade.

chofa: Half chair, half sofa. All mistake.

cleanser: Not as abrasive as bar soap. This is what you want to use on your face.

corduroy: From the French *cord-du-roi* ("cloth of kings"). Soft, ribbed fabric. Not just for pants, but definitely not for underwear.

couture: To clothing what Crystal is to Freixenet. Traditionally refers to highest of high fashion but used colloquially for all that is good in the sartorial arts.

couture splatter: Damage to clothing laid out for you by five visiting homosexuals. Also: The sad result of cooking without an apron.

crack: Unfortunate view when low-rise pants meet no-rise underwear. Crack is whack.

creative black tie: Vague direction affixed to some party invitation by well-meaning but clueless hosts, because it's often misinterpreted as an invitation to dress like a jackass, which clearly should not be the intent.

crew neck: Collarless collar as on a T-shirt, not to be confused with a TAB COLLAR, which is only for the confused.

dean-licious: Delicious, in the manner of James Dean.

destraightening: Phase of the show in which the straight subject is broken of his bad habits.

dimmer: Controls the brightness of lights. Put one on every possible light fixture in your house.

diuretics: Not to be confused with L. Ron Hubbard's religion, these are pills that help the body rid itself of excess fluids.

double-breasted: Style of suit with a lot of buttons and a lot of room for looking like an extra from *My Cousin Vinnie*. Tailored models can be very classy, but tread carefully: not for amateurs.

d.r.i.: Disco Related Injury. See also HETERO ARHYTHMIA.

electrostimulation: Rejuvenating treatment for skin without injections—a.k.a. "crunches for the face."

emollients: The natural oils in your skin that you want the proper levels of, or you end up looking like a vintage leather jacket.

empathy: Listening your way to getting lucky.

emulsify: 1. Warm up a hair product in your hands. 2. Using a whisk, food processor, or immersion blender, thoroughly mix the ingredients for a vinaigrette salad dressing or homemade mayonnaise. Don't confuse the two definitions.

exfoliation: Removing the dead layer of outer skin on your face so your skin looks better. To be done with a special product called an exfoliant, not with coarse sandpaper or a woodworking rasp.

fab five: Stylish and savvy saviors of straightness.

facial: Professional tough-love, pore-opening cleansing for your face.

fashion denim: Hybrid of classic denim shapes with high-concept bells-and-whistles, like rhinestones. Not for amateurs.

flat front: Pants without pleats, the way God intended them.

fleet week: On the town, in naval uniform.

flocking: Raised patterns on clothing.

follicle: The physiological structure that anchors individual strands of hair to your body—sort of ultra-miniature underground missile silos. The ones in the face can become irritated due to improper shaving technique.

free radicals: Naturally occurring substances that are dangerous to your complexion. Avoid as much as possible.

french cuffs: Shirt double-cuffs that close with removable links instead of buttons.

gay: Oh, do you mean QUEER?

gay kool-ade: Cocktail composed of Absolut vodka and soda with just enough cranberry to tint it pink.

gel: Product for controlling hair.

gewürtztraminer: Unpronounceable German white wine.

gin: Clear alcohol known for taste of juniper berries and causing violent hangovers.

"good times": Generic faux-nostalgic, semi ironic aside.

hair spray: The embalming fluid of hair control. Not to be used, unless you're working some advanced multi-product three-stage styling extravaganza, in which case you're a professional, in which case you're not reading this book. So, to reiterate: Not to be used.

hermès: French purveyors of saddlery, scarves, and other hot stuff that costs more than good-sized parcels of waterfront real estate.

hetero arhythmia: Straight men's chronic inability to dance.

horrendo: Short for horrendous. Used when something's just too horrendo to say the whole word.

jackass: What we're trying to prevent you from being.

julienne: Long, thin strips of food, usually vegetables. Also called matchsticks, but julienne sounds better.

knitware: Cotton, wool, or silk couture.

lapels: The suit's "wings." Yours shouldn't flap or fly around. This is where politicians often wear their American-flag pins.

licensed practitioners of fierceness: See FAB FIVE.

low rise: Pants with a shorter-than-normal distance between crotch and waist. Can be fashionable, but see CRACK.

man bag: Any kind of manly purse such as a messenger bag or a leather strappy number.

manicure: Put the man into manicure: Clean up your nails and cuticles.

man quiche: Italian torte, which is the real-man version of quiche.

manscaping: The gentle art of trimming your natural but unnecessary and unsightly masculine fur, like that pelt you're wearing on your back.

mise-en-place: Culinary term, from the French for having your shit together.

moisturizer: For any part of your body that's dry, especially your face.

monobrow: a.k.a. UNIBROW. Eyebrows that connect.

muddling: Gently mashing fruit or mint leaves for a cocktail.

nose hair: Ugly and unnecessary nasal love patch. Trim 'em.

paint-on architecture: Adding depth and drama to a room with just a coat of paint, often applied in different colors in selective areas, to provide architectural elements where none exists in your crappy Post-Modern pre-fab.

pedicure: Makeover for your toenails. Important for sandal season.

placket: Part of a dress shirt where the buttons go.

pleats: Extra fabric front on a pair of pants that supersizes the pelvis (in a bad way) and doesn't look good on anybody (including you).

pomade: A hair product that adds weight and shine but not a lot of hold, separation, or texture. Probably best if you wait until your stylist suggests it to you.

pores: Microscopic holes in your skin. Can become clogged if improperly cleaned.

pre-shave oil: Lubricant applied before shaving cream.

queer: Come on, people, you know this one.

razor burn: Red, inflamed skin as a result of an improper shaving technique.

sack suit: American suit style. Think Ivy League, or Kennedys in Camelot, not burlap.

sommelier: From the French for "the humiliator," but can—and should—be your friend: the guy who helps you choose the right wine for your food without breaking your budget. Consult him.

spf: Sun Protection Factor.

tab collar: The buttoning non-collar collar. Loserly. See also HORRENDO or TRAJICISTAN.

tannarexic: Begs the question, can one be too tan or too skinny? Probably, yes.

texturized cut: Hair cut at different lengths to reveal texture.

texturizing cream: Hair product for bringing out texture.

thom-trim: v., Similar to PAINT-ON ARCHITECTURE, a cool design thing that Thom made up and, with the extraordinary modesty and self-deprecation for which he's internationally famous, named after himself.

ticket pocket: Third pocket above side pockets on some suits. Not much practical use, but looks good and adds a level of sartorial flair.

trajicistan: Coming from a place of severely bad taste.

tszuj, tszujing: v. Finesse, tweak, rearrange, and make better. Garmento-speak co-opted by Carson, possibly of Yiddish origin.

unibrow: See MONOBROW.

vermouth: Necessary ingredient for the creation of a martini cocktail.

wax, hair: Sticky hair-holding product. You need to know what you're doing, guys.

waxing: Painful but often necessary procedure for the removal of unwanted hair from the back, chest, and . . . elsewhere.

witch hazel: Natural astringent. See ASTRINGENT.

acknowledgments

First of all, thanks to the extraordinarily skilled Adam Sachs, who not only helped us find the right words, but did it while impeccably dressed.

Of course, this book would not have been possible if the show weren't the greatest thing since sliced baguette topped with tapenade. For that, we have to thank our visionary and talented producers at Scout: creator/executive producer David Collins; executive producers David Metzler and Michael Williams; supervising producer Lynn Sadofsky; our personal Fab 5 producer, Michelle Platt; and to Kenya Miles, David Tamarkin, Bryan Lasseter, and Jamie O'Donnell for all of their assistance. Thank you to the superstar development team at Scout: Sean Baker, Brian Robel, and Ed Peselman. Special thanks to Dia Sokol, who coordinated everything with unshakeable cheer.

And especially thanks to Rob Eric, who did so much on this book that it would take pages to explain it.

To Brian Lipson and Greg Horangic, our agents at Endeavor, for finding the best publisher and putting all the pieces together.

And enormous thanks to Chris Pavone at Clarkson Potter: His vision, commitment, and advice made this book a reality.

Also to the whole team at Clarkson Potter and Crown, including Jenny Frost, Lauren Shakely, Philip Patrick, Tina Constable, Leigh Ann Ambrosi, Doug Jones, Adina Steiman, and everybody else who helped turn a book by five gay men into a major publishing event. To Mark McCauslin and Felix Gregorio, for copyediting and production. And especially to creative director Marysarah Quinn and designer Jan Derevjanik, for making this into a beautiful thing.

To photographers Quentin Bacon, Matt Albiani, Mark Ferri, Chris Haston, Scott Gries, and Craig Blankenhorn; and to stylists Alison Attenborough, Denise Carter, and Deborah Watson.

Special thanks to Jeff Gaspin, Ed Wilson, Bob Wright, and Jeff Zucker.

The day-to-day team who worked together to bring this project to fruition: Frances Berwick, April Brock, Lauren McCollester, Kim Niemi, George Nunes, Vivi Zigler, Lorey D. Zlotnick.

A project of this magnitude is truly a collaborative effort, and we would like to thank the many people at NBC and Bravo who gave their time and energies so generously including: Stephen Andrade, Christian Barcellos, Bill Brennan, Jenness Brewer, BJ Carretta, Marc Graboff, Jon Hookstratten, Amy Introcaso-Davis, Stacey Irvin, Loretta Kraft, Nancy McDyer, Jerry Petry, David Pai-Ritchie, Mitch Salem, Alan Seiffert, Jennifer Skorlich, and Eric Van Der Werff.

Finally, and most important, we'd like to thank everybody who has embraced the show, and especially the straight guys who've welcomed a little gay fabulosity into their lives. Cheers!

photography and styling credits

Front Matter

Page 2: Photograph by Chris Haston, copyright © 2003 by Bravo; styling by Carson Kressley, hair and makeup provided by Tracey Taylor.

Page 5, from left: Ted's suit by Versus, shirt and tie by Gucci; Thom's suit by Vestimenta, shirt by Etro, shoes by Via Spiga; Carson's suit by Roberto Cavalli and shirt by Calvin Klein; Jai's suit by Dolce & Gabbana; Kyan's suit and shirt by Jil Sander. Photograph by Craig Blankenhorn, copyright © 2003 by Bravo; styling by Carson Kressley.

Page 9: Photograph by Chris Haston, copyright © 2003 by Bravo; styling by Carson Kressley, hair and makeup provided by Tracey Taylor. *From left:* Dave Metzler's shirt by John Varvatos, pants by Prada, watch by Paul Smith; Dave Collins's shirt by Comme des Garçons, pants by Neil Barrett, watch by Diesel.

Page 10, clockwise from top: Ted's suit by Jil Sander, shirt by Byblos; Carson's velvet jacket by Gucci, pink shirt by Cherry Vintage, purple shirt by Piombo; Kyan's T-shirt and jeans by Roberto Cavalli; Jai's orange jacket by Jil Sander. Photograph by Craig Blankenhorn, copyright © 2003 by Bravo; styling by Carson Kressley.

Part 1: Food and Wine

Food photography by Quentin Bacon Studio, copyright © 2003; food styling by Alison Attenborough; prop styling by Denise Carter.

Still-life photography by Quentin Bacon Studio, copyright © 2003; still-life styling by Denise Carter.

Photographs on pages 14, 49, 78-79, by Craig Blankenhorn, copyright © 2003 by Bravo; styling by Carson Kressley.

Page 14: Pinstripe suit and orange shirt by Etro.

Page 21, from top: Chef's knife by Henkel; instant-read meat thermometer by Taylor; tongs by OXO; sauté pan by All-Clad.

Page 22, from top: Roasting pan by All-Clad; enamel-coated cast-iron pot by Le Creuset; pepper mill courtesy Broadway Panhandler.

Page 23, from top: Cast-iron skillet courtesy Quentin Bacon Studio; digital timer by Williams Sonoma.

Pages 24-25: Pyrex mixing bowls courtesy Broadway Panhandler.

Pages 26-27: All knives by Wüstohf.

Page 34, from top: "Rabbit" corkscrew by Metrokane; stainless-steel cocktail shaker courtesy Broadway Panhandler.

Page 49, from left: Ted's suit by Versus, shirt and tie by Gucci; Thom's suit by Vestimenta, shirt by Etro, shoes by Via Spiga; Carson's suit by Roberto Cavalli, shirt by Calvin Klein; Jai's suit by Dolce & Gabbana; Kyan's suit and shirt by Jil Sander.

Pages 78-79: Suit by Jil Sander, shirt by Byblos.

Part 2: Grooming

Still-life photography by Quentin Bacon Studio, copyright © 2003; still-life styling by Denise Carter.

Photographs on pages 86, 97, and 103 by Craig Blankenhorn, copyright © 2003 by Bravo; styling by Carson Kressley.

Photograph on page 110-11 by Michael Larsen, copyright © 2003 by Larsen & Talbert/ Icon International; styling by Susie Crippen, set design by John Millhauser, grooming by Jennifer Pitt.

Photograph on page 113 by Gilles Larraine, copyright © 2003.

Page 86: Leather shirt by Roberto Cavalli.

Page 90: Comb courtesy Denise Carter.

Page 93, top: Gel by Aura. *Bottom:* Cream by Bumble and Bumble.

Pages 94-95, clockwise from top right: Pomade by Aveda; hairspray by Phytolaque; wax by Bumble and Bumble.

Page 97: T-shirt by Roberto Cavalli.

Page 98: Turbo 5.0 nose-hair trimmer courtesy The Sharper Image.

Page 101: Tweezers by Tweezerman.

Page 103: Leather shirt and pants by Roberto Cavalli.

Pages 106-7: Facial cleanser by Aveda.

Page 108: Shaving cream by The Art of Shaving.

Page 113: Shaving set by E-Shave.

Page 117: Scissors by International Cutlery.

Part 3: Decorating

Still-life photography by Quentin Bacon Studio, copyright © 2003; still-life styling by Denise Carter.

Photographs on pages 118 and 134 by Craig Blankenhorn, copyright © 2003 by Bravo; styling by Carson Kressley.

Location photography on pages 122-23, 124-25, 128-29, 131, 132-33, 144-45, 146-47, and 151 by Mark Ferri, copyright © 2003.

Location photography on pages 136-37, 140-42, and 149 by Scott Gries.

Location photography on pages 152-59 by Craig Blankenhorn.

Page 118: Shirt and jacket by Etro.

Pages 120–21: Vases provided by Baker.

Pages 122-23: All furniture provided by Baker.

Pages 124-25: Stools, kitchen island, cart, and refrigeration unit provided by Balthaup; sofa, lamps, table, chairs provided by Baker.

Page 127: Shields and copper masks provided by Baker.

Pages 128-29: Kitchen island provided by Balthaup; wine unit designed by John Paino and Thom Filicia, built by Creative Engineering.

Page 131, top: Drawing by John Paino. *Bottom:* All furniture provided by Baker; TV unit built by Creative Engineering.

Pages 132-33: Kitchen island, stools, refrigeration unit provided by Balthaup; fireplace built by Creative Engineering.

Page 135: Candles by Pottery Barn.

Pages 136-37: All furniture provided by Baker.

Pages 138-39, clockwise from top left: Paint can courtesy Denise Carter; level by Stanley; Mirado Black Warrior pencil; roller and pad courtesy Janovic Plaza.

Pages 140-41: All furniture provided by Baker.

Page 142: All furniture provided by Baker.

Page 143, top: Vase by Room, New York City. *Bottom:* Vase by Baker.

Pages 144-45: All furniture provided by Baker.

Pages 146-47: All furniture provided by Baker.

Page 149: Art provided by Baker.

Page 151: Painting by Anya Spielman; urn and bench by Baker.

Pages 152-53: Patchwork club chair and all furniture by Thomasville; rug by Crate and Barrel.

Pages 154-55: Table designed and built by Jeff Toale; all other furniture by Thomasville; rug by Crate and Barrel.

Page 156-57: Guitars and pheasant courtesy Jeff Toale; all other furniture provided by Thomasville.

Pages 158-59, left: Table, chairs, chandelier provided by Thomasville; pheasant by Jeff Toale. *Right:* Quilt provided by Toale family.

Part 4: Fashion

Primary fashion photography by Matt Albiani, copyright © 2003; styling by Deborah Watson.

Photographs on pages 160, 170, 197, and 207 by Craig Blankenhorn, copyright © 2003 by Bravo; styling by Carson Kressley.

Pages 160: Velvet jacket by Gucci, pink shirt by Cherry Vintage, purple shirt by Piombo.

Pages 164-65, from left: 1. Gray wool pinstripe suit by Hugo Boss; belt and shirt by Polo Ralph Lauren. 2. Denim jacket by Levi's; T-shirt by John Varvatos; tan cargo pants by Abercrombie & Fitch. 3. Vintage cowboy boots from Melet Mercantile. 4. Green cashmere sweater and shirt by Polo Ralph Lauren. 5. Navy blazer, shirt, repp necktie, pocket square, and gray wool pants, all by Polo Ralph Lauren.

Page 167: Striped shirt by Paul Smith; necktie by Etro; silver and blue enamel cuff links by Brooks Brothers.

Page 169: All shirts by Polo Ralph Lauren except: Paisley shirt by Etro. Multicolored striped shirt by Paul Smith. Gray shirt by John Varvatos.

Page 170: Leather jacket by Roberto Cavalli, T-shirt by Von Dutch, jeans by Sheragano, shoes by Ralph Lauren.

Page 173: 1. Striped shirt by Paul Smith; necktie by Etro gray wool pants by Ralph Lauren Purple Label. 2. Striped shirt by Paul Smith; jeans by Paper Denim & Cloth. 3. Striped shirt by Paul Smith; black corduroy blazer by Polo Ralph Lauren; T-shirt by John Varvatos; tan cargo pants by Abercrombie & Fitch. 4. Striped shirt by Paul Smith; navy cashmere V-neck sweater by Burberry; tan corduroy pants by Seven.

Page 174: 1. Shirt, herringbone jacket, and gray wool pants by Polo Ralph Lauren. 2. Shirt and green cashmere sweater by Polo Ralph Lauren; chinos by Brooks Brothers; striped ribbon belt by J. Crew. 3. Shirt and jeans by Polo Ralph Lauren; blue thermal shirt by John Varvatos. 4. Shirt, belt, and pocket square by Polo Ralph Lauren; suit by Hugo Boss.

Pages 176-77: 1. Striped shirt by Paul Smith; blue necktie by Etro. 2. Light blue shirt by Brooks Brothers; black necktie by Ralph Lauren Purple Label. 3. Gray pinstripe suit by Louis Vuitton; white-collar shirt by Polo Ralph Lauren; necktie by Polo Ralph Lauren.

Pages 178-79, top: Distressed leather messenger bag by John Varvatos; herringbone jacket by Ralph Lauren Purple Label; jeans by Rogan. *Bottom:* Denim jacket by Levi's; T-shirt by John Varvatos; aviator sunglasses by Ray-Ban.

Page 180: Rolex Submariner watch.

Page 181: All pocket squares by Ralph Lauren Purple Label. All cuff links by Brooks Brothers.

Page 183, from top: Brown wingtips by Polo Ralph Lauren; black cap-toe dress shoes by Polo Ralph Lauren; suede driving moccasins by Tod's; Converse All-Star sneakers; vintage cowboy boots from Melet Mercantile.

Pages 184-85: Jeans by Polo Ralph Lauren.

Page 186, clockwise from top left: "Classic" jeans by Levi's "Austin"; "Boot-Cut" jeans by Paper Denim & Cloth; "Relaxed" jeans by Rogan; "Low-Rise" jeans by Chip & Pepper.

Page 187: "Fashion" jeans by Dolce & Gabbana.

Page 188: Vintage denim jacket by Levi's.

Page 189: Flip-flops by Havaianas.

Pages 190-91: Striped shirt by Paul Smith, necktie by Etro, gray wool suit by Polo Ralph Lauren.

Page 192, top: Single-breasted, one-button gray pinstripe suit by Giorgio Armani; gray wool shirt by John Varvatos; necktie by Giorgio Armani. Bottom: Single-breasted, two-button gray pinstripe suit by Hugo Boss; shirt, tie, and pocket square by Ralph Lauren Purple Label.

Page 193, top: Single-breasted, three-button gray herringbone suit, blue oxford, necktie, and pocket square, all by Polo Ralph Lauren. Bottom: Double-breasted gray suit, satin tie, and pocket square by Ralph Lauren Purple Label; striped shirt by Paul Smith.

Page 196: Gray pinstripe suit by Louis Vuitton; white-collar shirt and knit tie by Polo Ralph Lauren.

Page 197, from left: Ted's suit by Versus, shirt and tie by Gucci; Thom's suit by Vestimenta, shirt by Etro, shoes by Via Spiga; Carson's suit by Roberto Cavalli and shirt by Calvin Klein; Jai's suit by Dolce & Gabbana; Kyan's suit and shirt by Jil Sander.

Pages 198-99: 1. Shawl-collar tuxedo by Ralph Lauren; shirt and pocket square by Polo Ralph Lauren; antique black-enamel stud set from Barneys New York. 2. Peak-lapel tuxedo by Polo Ralph Lauren; shirt and pocket square by Polo Ralph Lauren; bowtie by Barneys New York; sterling silver stud set by Barneys New York. 3. Notch-collar tuxedo by Polo Ralph Lauren; shirt and pocket square by Ralph Lauren Purple Label; bowtie by Barneys New York; black-enamel stud set by Brooks Brothers.

Pages 200-1: Sterling silver cuff-link knots by Barneys New York; tuxedo and shirt by Polo Ralph Lauren.

Pages 202-3: Herringbone blazer, striped shirt, knit tie, pocket square, and wool pants, all by Polo Ralph Lauren.

Page 204: Herringbone blazer, sweater, and pocket square by Polo Ralph Lauren; jeans by Paper Denim & Cloth.

Page 205, clockwise from top left: Navy blazer by Polo Ralph Lauren; pink shirt, gray repp necktie, and pocket square by Polo Ralph Lauren. Navy blazer by Polo Ralph Lauren; T-shirt courtesy of Barneys New York; jeans by Rogan. Navy blazer by Polo Ralph Lauren; shirt by Paul Smith; vintage denim jacket by Levi's; tan corduroy pants by Seven. Navy blazer by Polo Ralph Lauren; gray cashmere hooded sweatshirt by Polo Ralph Lauren; chinos by Brooks Brothers; striped ribbon belt by J. Crew; watch by Rolex.

Page 207: Leather jacket by Roberto Cavalli, T-shirt by Von Dutch; jeans by Sheragano; shoes by Ralph Lauren.

Part 5: Culture

Still-life photography by Quentin Bacon Studio, copyright © 2003; still-life styling by Denise Canter.

Photographs on pages 208, 222, 233, 242 by Craig Blankenhorn, copyright © 2003 by Bravo; styling by Carson Kressley.

Photograph on pages 212-13 by Gary Buss/Getty Images.

Photograph on pages 234-35 by Photodisc Collections/Getty Images.

Photograph on page 237 by Hans Neleman/Photonica.

Photograph on page 241 by Davies + Starr/Getty Images.

Page 208: Suit and shirt by Roberto Cavalli.

Page 216: Stationery by Les Papiers Jean Rouget.

Page 219: Glass by Crate & Barrel.

Page 220: Champagne by Dom Pérignon.

Page 222: Suit and shirt by Roberto Cavalli.

Pages 224-25: Cell phone by Motorola.

Page 233, from left: Ted's suit by Versus, shirt and tie by Gucci; Jai's suit by Dolce & Gabbana; Carson's suit by Roberto Cavalli, shirt by Calvin Klein; Kyan's suit and shirt by Jil Sander; Thom's suit by Vestimenta, shirt by Etro, shoes by Via Spiga. Orange briefcase by Veii by Jeffrey Sperber.

Page 243: Suit and shirt by Roberto Cavalli; shoes by Diesel.

Back Matter

Page 248, from left: Kyan's leather shirt and pants by Roberto Cavalli; Ted's suit and shirt by Etro; Carson's leather jacket by Roberto Cavalli, T-shirt by Von Dutch, jeans by Sheragano, shoes by Ralph Lauren; Jai's suit and shirt by Roberto Cavalli; Thom's shirt and jacket by Etro. Photograph by Craig Blankenhorn, copyright © 2003 by Bravo; styling by Carson Kressley.

index